CHIEFS KINGDOM

THE OFFICIAL STORY OF THE 2019 CHAMPIONSHIP SEASON

CHIEFS KINGDOM

THE OFFICIAL STORY OF THE 2019 CHAMPIONSHIP SEASON

FOREWORD BY ANDY REID

EDITED BY MICHAEL MacCAMBRIDGE

Andrews McMeel
PUBLISHING®

Front cover: Chiefs' offense huddles during Sept. 22, 2019, game against Baltimore at Arrowhead Stadium.

Front endsheets: Opening kickoff at Arrowhead Stadium, Nov. 3, 2019.

Pages 2–3: Travis Kelce during pregame introductions at AFC Championship Game, Jan. 19, 2020.

Pages 4–5: The Chiefs defense takes a break during the 28–10 win over Oakland, Sept. 15, 2019.

Pages 6–7: Damien Williams scores the Chiefs' first touchdown in AFC Divisional Playoff Game, Jan. 12, 2020.

Page 8: Patrick Mahomes prior to the Chiefs game with Houston, Oct. 13, 2019.

Page 136–137: Frank Clark admires postgame confetti; special teams coordinator Dave Toub accepts congratulations; Patrick Mahomes and Travis Kelce celebrate in locker room; Tyrann Mathieu on the victory podium; Mecole Hardman and Byron Pringle snap a selfie; Norma and Clark Hunt with the Lombardi Trophy; Derrick Nnadi makes a confetti angel.

Page 138–139: Tammy and Andy Reid on the parade bus; the crowd converged on the parade's conclusion at Union Station; Frank Clark and Travis Kelce on the stage; the players shared in the crowd's euphoria; Clark Hunt raises the Lombardi Trophy; the Sprint Center sported a championship banner; parade buses made their way through downtown Kansas City.

Back endsheets: Pregame at Arrowhead Stadium, Oct. 6, 2019.

Back cover: Tyrann Mathieu, flanked by Rashad Fenton, Armani Watts, Daniel Sorensen, and Ben Niemann, celebrates after interception against Los Angeles Chargers, Dec. 29, 2019.

Chiefs Kingdom copyright © 2020 by 24/7 Publishing LLC. All rights reserved. Printed in China. No part of this book may be used or reproduced in any manner whatsoever without written permission except in the case of reprints in the context of reviews.

Andrews McMeel Publishing
a division of Andrews McMeel Universal
1130 Walnut Street, Kansas City, Missouri 64106

www.andrewsmcmeel.com

20 21 22 23 24 TEN 10 9 8 7 6 5 4 3 2 1
ISBN: 978-1-5248-6478-1
Library of Congress Control Number: 2020939520

Editor: Jean Z. Lucas
Art Director: Spencer Williams
Production Manager: Carol Coe
Production Editor: Dave Shaw

Photography: Steve Sanders, team photographer Kansas City Chiefs.
Additional photography: Jim Berry, Andrew Mather, Ben Green, Chris Donahue, Sam Lutz, Cassie Florido, Evan Sanders, Aaron Sprecher.

ATTENTION: SCHOOLS AND BUSINESSES
Andrews McMeel books are available at quantity discounts with bulk purchase for educational, business, or sales promotional use. For information, please e-mail the Andrews McMeel Publishing Special Sales Department: specialsales@amuniversal.com.

For those who will
always remember
February 2, 2020
. . . and January 11, 1970

FOREWORD

BY ANDY REID

I still remember the day I realized I was going to become the head coach of the Kansas City Chiefs. It was January 2, 2013, in a conference room inside the Philadelphia airport. I'd recently been fired by the Philadelphia Eagles, but I knew I wanted to coach again.

The Chiefs were one of the teams that were interested in interviewing me, and Clark Hunt showed up with a good portion of the front office. I'd always held the Hunt family in high regard; my wife, Tammy, had gotten to know Norma Hunt during our time in the league, and I'd felt for a while that if I ever went somewhere else, the Chiefs would be one of the teams I'd be interested in, because of the family and the way they go about business. Also, my friend Dick Vermeil—revered in both Philadelphia and Kansas City—raved about his time coaching the Chiefs.

During the interview that day, it became clear that Clark and I wanted the same things, and could forge a good working relationship. The conversations just kept going; two hours turned into four hours, and four turned into six, and the interview wound up lasting nine hours. By about hour seven I was comfortable enough to call my wife and say, "Listen, I think we're a pretty good way along here, and this sounds like it's going to be the right place."

I already knew about the Chiefs' fan base and Arrowhead Stadium. In the late '80s and early '90s, while I was on the staff at the University of Missouri, I'd drive up from Columbia to spend time with the irascible Howard Mudd, Marty Schottenheimer's offensive line coach for his early Chiefs teams. Everything about the gameday experience there was terrific: the stadium was clean and classy, the crowd was loud and supportive, and the people were incredibly friendly. You could tell that football was an important part of the community.

Coaches are teachers but they also need to learn themselves. By the time I got to Kansas City in 2013, I was older and more experienced. I was not quite as rigid as I had been in Philadelphia. I was pretty stern at the beginning of my time there, and had been a little more standoffish with the media. But as the team grew, I grew with them, and by the time I took the job in Kansas City, I had walked in those moccasins before.

So I was probably more relaxed, but I still kept high expectations for the team. We were fortunate that there was already a good core of leaders on the team—people like Eric Berry, Derrick Johnson, and Tamba Hali. And their desire to win was clear; the message I got from those players was, "Just tell us what we need to do, and we'll do it."

So we all went to work. I felt like we needed a quarterback here, and I'd always been a fan of Alex Smith, from the time he was in college. I felt he would get us

Nov. 3, 2019, game against Minnesota.

Introductory press conference, Jan. 7, 2013, with Chiefs Chairman Clark Hunt.

going and competing for championships. He had the talents you want in a quarterback, but also the personality. He was the ultimate professional: the hardest worker, always in the best shape, and the smartest guy we had, and he brought it every day. He's a good-looking guy, too, but amazingly tough underneath those blue eyes.

Right from the beginning, you could feel something special happening. Arrowhead set the Guinness Book world record for being the loudest stadium in the world in 2013, against the Raiders, and again in 2014, against the Patriots. Watching something like that on TV doesn't really do it justice. There was a vibration on the field that I've never felt anywhere else, where the fans cranked it up to higher decibel levels than what they'd managed in Seattle, and the ground was shaking.

As we continued to build a perennial contender in Kansas City, one of the key components, of course, was Patrick Mahomes, about whom Brett Veach had argued for so passionately before the draft in 2017. Patrick had the makings of a great quarterback already, but he'll be the first to tell you that he had a great example to follow in Alex Smith. What he learned watching Alex that first year allowed Patrick to excel in his first season as the starter in 2018. Within the team, we knew what he was capable of; we'd seen it in training camp and at practices. So we were pleased but not surprised with his MVP season in 2018. We came so close that year, falling just short in overtime to the Patriots in the AFC Championship Game. But we'd learned something about ourselves in the process: We knew we could play with anybody.

•

At the beginning of the 2019 season, I didn't want the guys to forget the painful feeling of that narrow loss, not that they would. I mentioned it just a couple of times—at the beginning of OTAs, and again at training camp. I said, "We were four inches short last year, but we were all four inches short. Now we have to all get a little bit better, and take it up a notch." Then I just left it alone. The players knew, and they'd done the work in the off-season, and showed up ready to go.

Brett Veach had done a brave, phenomenal job of rebuilding our defense by bringing in leaders like Tyrann

Mathieu and Frank Clark. The defense really improved over the course of the season with Steve Spagnuolo in charge. On offense, Eric Bieniemy did a terrific job—even though it seemed like nearly everyone on that side of the ball was banged up at one point or another during the season—and so did Dave Toub, one of the best special teams coordinators ever. When all three phases contribute, good things usually happen.

Seasons almost always have ups and downs. Everybody deals with injuries; that's part of the game. When Patrick got injured against the Broncos, we had the benefit of a truly great medical staff—including head trainer Rick Burkholder and team doctor Paul Schroeppel—who took quick, decisive action. And Matt Moore rose to the occasion in Pat's absence. It was similar to what Mike Livingston had done 50 years earlier, in 1969, when Len Dawson was injured the season the Chiefs won their first Super Bowl.

Our toughest point of the season actually came later, after Pat returned. It was the game at Tennessee where we lost to the Titans and fell to 6-4. We all had a piece of that. Every unit had a chance to win that game—the offense, the defense, and the special teams each had an opportunity to put that game away—and we all fell short.

So, heading into the following week's game, against the Chargers in Mexico City, everyone on the team knew it was going to be a pivotal game, not just because it was on Monday Night Football in Mexico City, but because of the situation we'd put ourselves in. We didn't have much margin for error. I explained to our guys that Estadio Azteca was going to feel a little like a playoff game, with that kind of atmosphere and constant noise. It was going to be a brawl to the end, and it was. What an effort; the thin air was brutal, and guys were dying in that altitude, but they pushed themselves through it. After the way they attacked the game and prevailed, I felt like we were going to be all right.

You have to be good in the NFL. But you have to be fortunate as well. And we got a break when Ryan Fitzpatrick led the Dolphins to an upset win over the Patriots on the last Sunday of the regular season, earning us a bye.

In that first playoff game against the Texans, everything that could go wrong at the beginning of the game did, but even when we were down 24–0, I never felt panicked, and I never sensed it in the team. The feeling was more like, *This isn't us*. The whole team had a mindset of, if we just calm down, and pump the brakes, we can flip this thing around. That's how I felt, and that's how the guys felt. And when Mecole Hardman hit that big kickoff return, you could just sense, "Here we go."

That was another game where the Arrowhead crowd really made a difference. They didn't get down or lose faith. They'd been loud throughout the season, and now you get into the playoffs and it's cold, and yet it's still really loud. And that noise becomes an issue for opposing quarterbacks and guys trying to run their offense.

The week of the AFC Championship Game, we were focused on the game, but we also knew what was at stake. There was a trip to the Super Bowl, but there was also the symbolic significance of winning the Lamar Hunt Trophy. Clark Hunt had addressed the team in training camp, challenging them to get to the next level. Dick Vermeil had come in during the season, and talked to the guys as well. He was already in tears at the beginning of his talk, about how much he'd wanted to win the Lamar Hunt Trophy for the family and the fans, and how disappointed he was to not be able to do it. But by the end, he was in full coach mode, about how this team could achieve that goal.

It took a complete team effort to come back again and beat the Titans, but there was so much self-belief on the team by that time. Of all the scenes I remember afterward—the big celebration at Arrowhead with all the confetti—the one that was most touching was watching Norma Hunt as she kissed the Lamar Hunt Trophy.

Of course, we still had work to do. I'd been to enough Super Bowls to know that you want to keep things as close to normal as possible. We installed the game plan the first week. When we got to Miami, I knew I could trust the guys. I knew they'd handle themselves the right way and they did. There weren't any of the big distractions that can pop up during Super Bowl week.

During the week in Miami, I let some other people do most of the talking. I asked Donovan McNabb to come to practice, and he talked about getting to the game and not winning it. Brett Favre talked to the guys about winning one Super Bowl and losing another, and how precious those trips to the game were. Hall of Fame coach Jimmy Johnson spoke, out on the field after practice one day, about how much a win would mean to the players' lives. And Friday, Clark Hunt talked to the team, and told them how proud he was of what they'd already accomplished. The night before the game, I asked Terrell Suggs to speak. He was at the Super Bowl when he was young and they won the game.

I thought it was worthwhile to get some other voices in there, another flavor than just me, who'd been hacking on these guys for 20 weeks. I didn't speak long at all that Saturday night, but one of the things I told the guys is that every year is different, and every team is different. But I said if I could have this team, this group of guys right here together, I could coach another 30 years.

Then there was the game, and it had that element you always want in a Super Bowl, of two excellent teams, evenly matched, just leaving it all out on the field. One of the defining characteristics of our team is that they simply don't give up. And even when we had that interception in the fourth quarter, and the 49ers were up 10 points with the ball, our guys just kept grinding.

Then we get the ball back, and we're down 20–10 and facing a third-and-15, during a replay review, and Patrick was talking with Eric Bieniemy and asked about our play called "3 Jet Chip Wasp." We'd been talking the whole second half about when we might run it, and Patrick was right to ask if we had enough time against the fierce 49ers pass rush to let the route develop.

I already knew he wanted the play, and that's what we wound up calling. Patrick took what was basically a nine-step drop—which you don't see every day—and it worked. The cornerback on that side hugged down on Sammy Watkins when he turned in. And that left the free safety turning his hips in the expectation that Tyreek Hill was running a post route. It was a similar look to a play we'd run earlier called Bolt, and the 49ers probably thought we were going back to that again. Wasp complemented that play very well, and then Patrick got the throw off, even before Tyreek made his cut toward the sideline, so Tyreek was wide open when the ball arrived.

That helped get us back into the game, but then we had to keep making big plays. Chris Jones, who'd been injured much of the postseason, was immense, a really disruptive force on the line, knocking down balls in crucial situations. And then, when we got ahead and needed one more first down to ice it, our offensive line did a great job clearing some room for Damien Williams, and he took it to the house.

Afterward, the thing I remember best is just the sheer joy, going back and forth in every direction. I shared a hug with Patrick, my wife, and my boys, and that felt great. I was so happy for Clark Hunt and he was happy for me. I was thrilled for the guys on the team, and the staff, and the city. Most of the people on the field have been playing football or coaching football their whole lives, and this was the ultimate. At the parade, you got a strong sense of just how much it meant to the city.

It's a great accomplishment, and it goes beyond the stars. Patrick Mahomes and Tyreek Hill and Travis Kelce and Tyrann Mathieu and Frank Clark and Chris Jones get all the notoriety, and they should, because they're all great players. But I don't know if people fully appreciate what a team effort this is, how every guy on the roster has to make an important contribution along the way. Just one example: Byron Pringle, a terrific special teams player but also someone who's coming into his own as a receiver, came in the game late at Detroit. On our final drive, he made a key catch for a first down, then absorbed a huge hit but didn't lose the ball. That play was crucial to the game, and the game was crucial to the season. If we don't win that game, we don't get the bye the first week of the playoffs. We had dozens of other instances across the season, of guys stepping up when we needed them most.

And it wasn't just the 53 guys on the team, it was everybody. Our equipment manager Allen Wright (whom I'd gotten to know back in '89 during my first visits to

After the Super Bowl, Feb. 2, 2020.

Arrowhead) did an amazing job getting the players outfitted with what they needed to play in a driving rainstorm against the Ravens in September, then a driving snowstorm against the Broncos in December. It went on even after we won the Super Bowl; our president, Mark Donovan, worked pretty much around the clock to set up that marvelous parade experience.

•

The relationships are what will last. I've seen some of these players on that '69 Chiefs team—all-time greats like Emmitt Thomas, Willie Lanier, Jan Stenerud, and Bobby Bell—and 50 years later, you can still sense the bond, the way it brought them together and still does, and how much it meant to them and to the city. I'm glad that the 2019 Chiefs will have that to look forward to in the years ahead.

But as I said at the parade, we're not done. I've talked to people who've won the Super Bowl multiple times and they all say the same thing: Once you win it, it doesn't lessen the hunger; instead, you want all the more to win it again. I know what they mean.

To finally win a Super Bowl as a head coach was great, but I don't think about it much in terms of me. You don't get into the game for fancy jewelry. You do it because it's a great game, and for that sense of camaraderie and teamwork. You do it because you love the process, and care about each other and the team and the fans.

So I'll never forget this season, and the story of it that you'll read in the pages to follow. But even though seasons end, the process of team-building doesn't. You're always looking ahead, to the next challenge, the next opportunity, the next chance to come together as a team. That's what I love most about the job. And why I'm so happy to be doing it here in Kansas City.

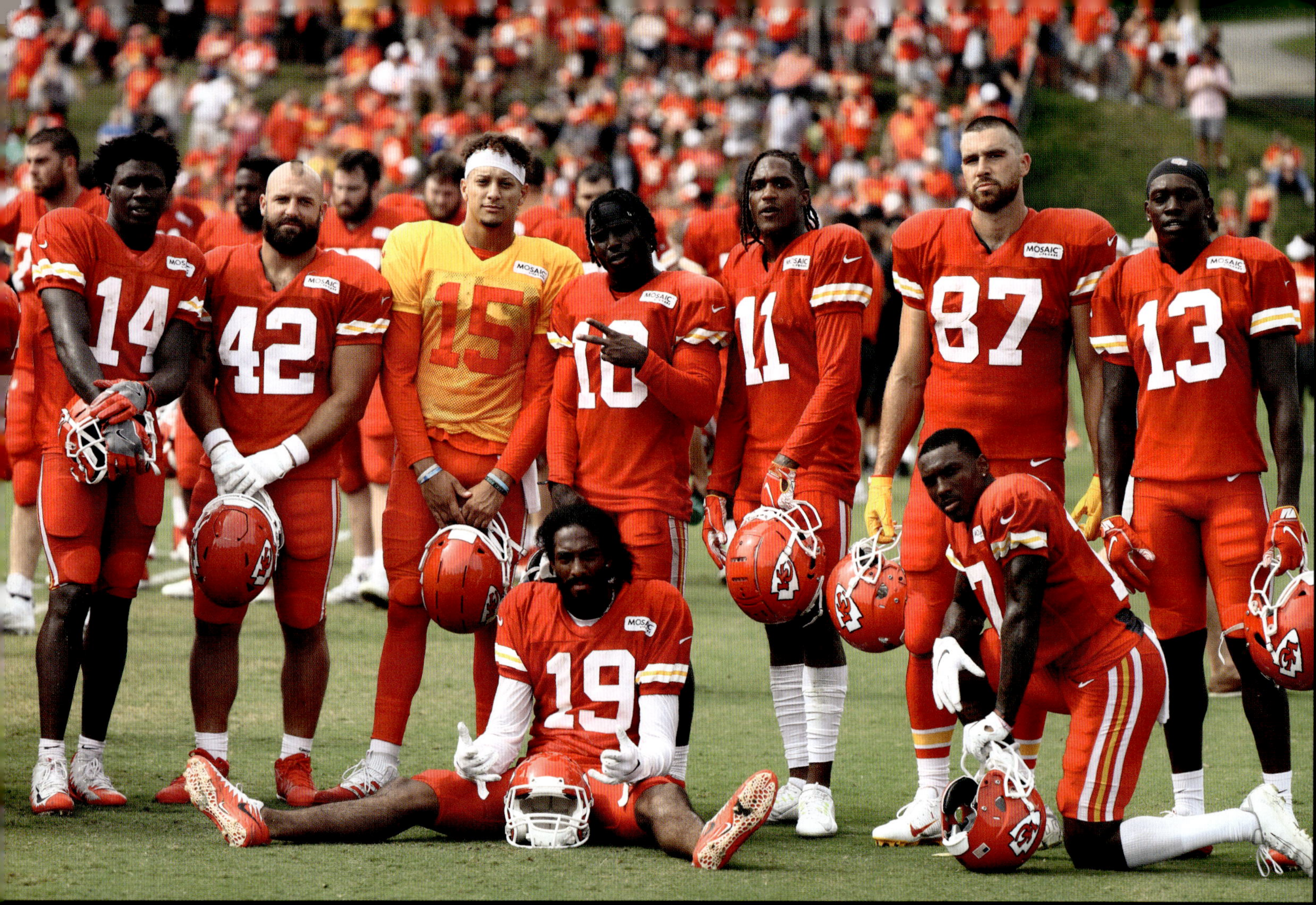

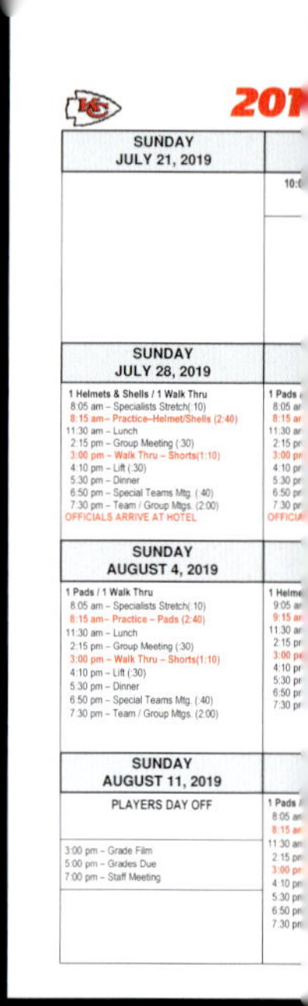
201

SUNDAY JULY 21, 2019
SUNDAY JULY 28, 2019
1 Helmets & Shells / 1 Walk Thru 8:05 am – Specialists Stretch(:10) 8:15 am– Practice–Helmet/Shells (2:40) 11:30 am – Lunch 2:15 pm – Group Meeting (:30) 3:00 pm – Walk Thru – Shorts(1:10) 4:10 pm – Lift (:30) 5:30 pm – Dinner 6:50 pm – Special Teams Mtg. (:40) 7:30 pm – Team / Group Mtgs. (2:00) OFFICIALS ARRIVE AT HOTEL
SUNDAY AUGUST 4, 2019
1 Pads / 1 Walk Thru 8:05 am – Specialists Stretch(:10) 8:15 am– Practice – Pads (2:40) 11:30 am – Lunch 2:15 pm – Group Meeting (:30) 3:00 pm – Walk Thru – Shorts(1:10) 4:10 pm – Lift (:30) 5:30 pm – Dinner 6:50 pm – Special Teams Mtg. (:40) 7:30 pm – Team / Group Mtgs. (2:00)
SUNDAY AUGUST 11, 2019
PLAYERS DAY OFF
3:00 pm – Grade Film 5:00 pm – Grades Due 7:00 pm – Staff Meeting

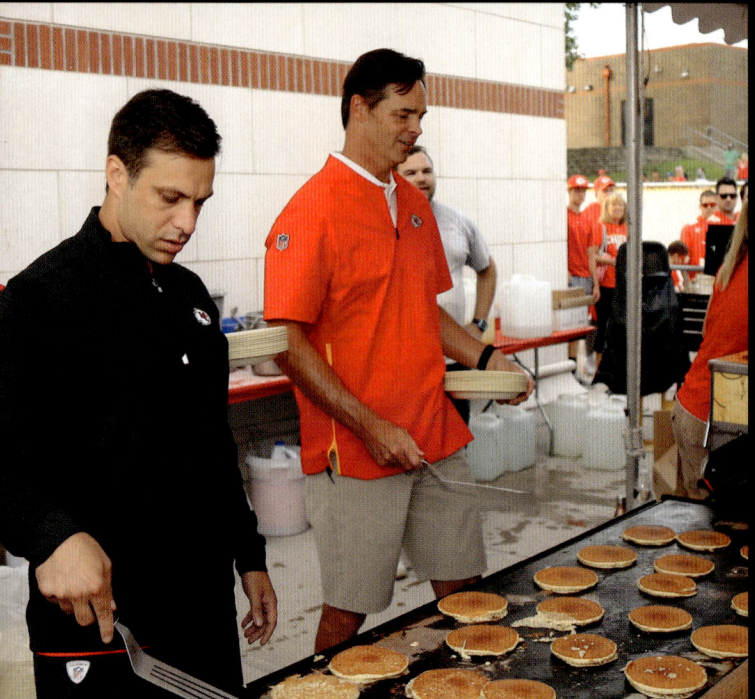

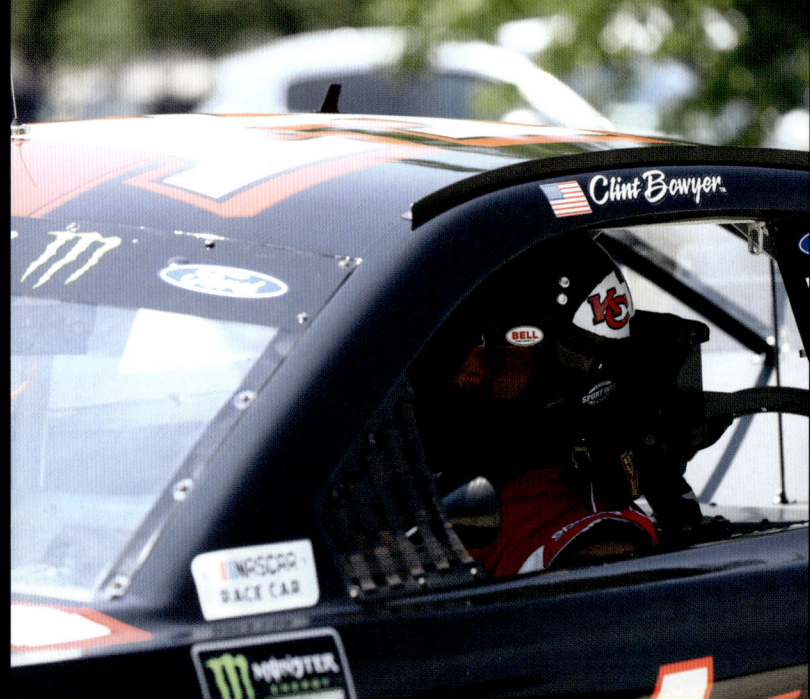

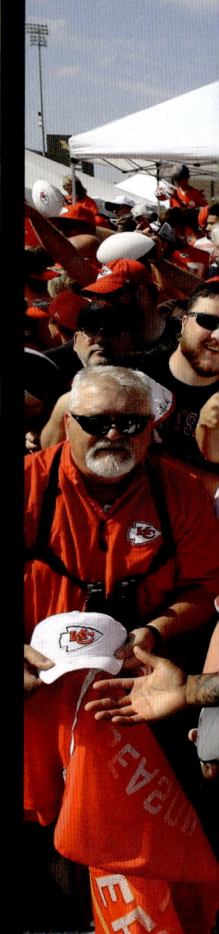

TRAINING CAMP AND PRESEASON

HIGH HOPES

The epic journey began on a stifling July day in St. Joseph, Missouri, as the three-time defending AFC West champion Chiefs returned to their training camp home on the campus of Missouri Western State University, faced with great expectations and a fair amount of uncertainty. Could the NFL's best offense continue its torrid run through the league? Would the retooled defense, under new coordinator Steve Spagnuolo, show significant improvement? And would 2019 be the season the Chiefs returned to the Super Bowl?

Clockwise from upper left: A moment of respite on the field; crowded camp schedule; Juan Thornhill with fans; Anthony Sherman arriving to camp; Brett Veach and Mark Donovan flipping flapjacks on Season Ticket Member Day.

"I like getting up here and getting everybody together. I like that camaraderie part of it, spending the time together. I'm not saying that you can't do it another way but I do like this way. I think Patrick [Mahomes] probably said it the best—it is a brotherhood. By the time you leave here, you're a family and then you keep building on that."

—HEAD COACH ANDY REID ON THE VALUE OF TRAINING CAMP

Clockwise from upper left: Mitchell Schwartz and Eric Fisher warm up; Ben Niemann; Steelers coach Mike Tomlin greets Frank Clark; 2020 schedule card; Chiefs gather in tunnel before preseason opener; Carlos Hyde scores a touchdown on the first offensive drive of 2019 preseason.

GAME 1 | SEPTEMBER 8, 2019, AT JACKSONVILLE

RISE AND SHINE
CHIEFS 40, JAGUARS 26

Two hundred and thirty-two days after the dream 2018 season ended with an all-too-familiar nightmare—a January playoff loss at Arrowhead—the retooled Chiefs embarked on a new journey, intent on getting a step further in the 2019 campaign. The league's most prolific offense struck early and often (scoring on its first seven drives) as defending league MVP Patrick Mahomes riddled the Jaguars for 378 yards passing, and wideout Sammy Watkins enjoyed a career day. Though injuries and defensive lapses would prove a concern, the runaway season-opening win showed a team picking up right where it left off.

On the season's third play, Watkins brought a short Mahomes pass 68 yards.

THE GAME STORY · The Chiefs jumped out to an early 10-point lead within the first nine minutes of the game, and despite an admirable performance by Jaguars' rookie backup quarterback Gardner Minshew, subbing for Nick Foles—who suffered a shoulder injury in the first quarter—Kansas City never relinquished its advantage.

Chiefs' quarterback Patrick Mahomes completed 25-of-33 passes for 378 yards and three scores, finding wide receiver Sammy Watkins for a pair of long touchdowns in the first half. Watkins's first score went for 68 yards before his second touchdown grab covered 49 yards down the sideline. It was all part of a career day for Watkins, who tallied 198 receiving yards and three scores on the afternoon.

The Jaguars found the end zone in between Watkins's two scores, but Harrison Butker went on to add three field goals for Kansas City to maintain the Chiefs' advantage heading into halftime.

The scoring slowed down in the second half, but Kansas City still managed to extend its lead as tailback Damien Williams burst ahead for a 1-yard score late in the third quarter. It marked Williams's 11th touchdown in his last seven games dating back to last season, and pushed the Chiefs' scoring total to at least 26 points for the 19th consecutive contest, matching an NFL record.

Williams's touchdown was set up by Kansas City's first takeaway of the season, as linebacker Damien Wilson punched the ball free from Jaguars' tailback Leonard Fournette and cornerback Bashaud Breeland scooped it up.

It was part of a solid overall showing for the Chiefs' new-look defense, which held Jacksonville to just 13 points until midway through the fourth quarter. Defensive end Frank Clark was part of that effort in his first game with Kansas City, picking off Minshew late in the game. It was the second interception of Clark's career.

Mahomes finished the contest with the second-most passing yards (378) and the second-highest passer rating (143.2) of his young career.

—MATT McMULLEN

"I can tell why he's MVP. He's special . . . I think what people don't understand is how smart he is. He can razzle-dazzle with his arm and his no-looks, but he's really intelligent."

—RUNNING BACK LeSEAN MCCOY,
AFTER HIS FIRST GAME WITH PATRICK MAHOMES

Tyrann Mathieu rallied the defense before kickoff.
2018 MVP Mahomes was back in midseason form.

"We didn't really put our best selves out on the field, but it was the first game—a lot of new players, new coaches, coming together, jelling at once. Overall, we did enough to get the win. Oh, man . . . we've got a lot of work to do."

—LINEBACKER DAMIEN WILSON

THE BIG PLAYS

1ST QUARTER, 13:36, 0-0 | CHIEFS BALL, 3RD & 3 AT KC 32
Patrick Mahomes hits Sammy Watkins in a seam; Watkins breaks a tackle and goes 68 yards to put the Chiefs ahead on the season's third play.

1ST QUARTER, 2:45, KC 10-7 | CHIEFS BALL, 1ST & 10 AT JAC 49
Mahomes finds Watkins all alone near the sideline, and hits him for a 49-yard touchdown pass to put the Chiefs back up by 10.

3RD QUARTER, 8:59, KC 23-13 | JAGUARS BALL, 3RD & 2 AT KC 26
With Jacksonville driving to make it a one-score game, Leonard Fournette catches a short pass and turns upfield, but the ball is stripped by Damien Wilson, and recovered by Bashaud Breeland.

The victory at Jacksonville elicited the season's first "How 'bout those . . . CHIEFS!" from Reid.

Kelce hauled in a touchdown pass during the second-quarter scoring explosion.

GAME 2 | SEPTEMBER 15, 2019, AT OAKLAND

DON'T CALL IT A COMEBACK

CHIEFS 28, RAIDERS 10

Rivalry week came early—a key AFC West showdown against the 1-0 Raiders. It was to be the last game the Chiefs would play at the stadium forever known (various corporate sponsors notwithstanding) as "Oakland–Alameda County Coliseum," and also likely the last NFL game ever played on a dirt infield. Though the Chiefs stumbled out of the gate, going down 10–0, matters were set right quickly and definitively, as Patrick Mahomes threw four touchdown passes in the second quarter, the Kansas City defense forced two turnovers in the second half, and the Chiefs left the Raiders in the (infield) dust.

> *"He had red in his eyes. He was telling us, 'Let's go out here and have a good quarter and get in the end zone. Lets just try to kill their pride.' He was hot then, he was dead-on every pass, and he definitely put it out there so that we can make a play."*
>
> —WIDE RECEIVER MECOLE HARDMAN, ON PATRICK MAHOMES'S SECOND QUARTER

THE GAME STORY · Oakland jumped out to a 10-point lead before Kansas City exploded for 28 points in the second quarter alone, as Chiefs' quarterback Patrick Mahomes passed for 278 yards and four touchdowns to establish a commanding advantage in a matter of minutes, and they never looked back.

Fourth-year wide out Demarcus Robinson caught two of those scores, hauling in a 44-yard grab to kick off the scoring and a 39-yard catch in the closing seconds of the first half. Rookie wide receiver Mecole Hardman also found the end zone during the quarter with a 42-yard touchdown—the first of his professional career—before tight end Travis Kelce brought in a 27-yard score.

Mahomes's 278 passing yards during the scoring barrage were the most in a single quarter since 2008 and his four scoring strikes were the most in a single quarter in franchise history. The performance also marked Mahomes's seventh straight road game with at least three touchdown passes, setting an NFL record.

The 23-year-old Mahomes went on to complete 30-of-44 passes for 443 yards and four touchdowns in the game, recording the second-most passing yards of his young career.

Robinson ended his day with a career-high six catches for 172 yards and two scores while Kelce also put together a strong game, catching seven passes for 107 yards and a touchdown.

Defensively, cornerbacks Bashaud Breeland and Charvarius Ward each had an interception, while cornerback Kendall Fuller, defensive end Tanoh Kpassagnon, and defensive lineman Chris Jones each notched a sack as Kansas City held Oakland scoreless following their early 10-point lead.

—MATT McMULLEN

The game in the NFL's 100th season also marked, likely, the last NFL game ever to be played on a dirt infield, and the Chiefs' last-ever trip to Oakland's stadium.

Robinson made some spectacular catches in a career-best 172-yard day.

Mahomes threw for 278 yards and four touchdowns in the second quarter alone.

THE BIG PLAYS

1ST QUARTER, 1:17, OAK 10–0 | RAIDERS BALL, 3RD & 8 AT OAK 42
Derek Carr's pass to Hunter Renfrow is defended by Kendall Fuller, forcing a Raider punt and keeping it a two-score game.

2ND QUARTER, 5:57, OAK 10–7 | CHIEFS BALL, 3RD & 20 AT OAK 42
Converting on third down for the fourth time in a 95-yard drive, Patrick Mahomes finds Mecole Hardman splitting the defense, for a 42-yard go-ahead score.

2ND QUARTER, 1:46, KC 14–10 | CHIEFS BALL, 2ND & 17 AT OAK 27
Mahomes lofts a perfectly-placed ball to Travis Kelce tightroping down the sideline, into double coverage, and Kelce holds on to it for a touchdown.

"When you come here, you've got to be a team. There is no place in the league—even though our fans snuck in here and they were great and we thank them for taking that chance because this is a tough place to come in. I was proud of our guys for doing that, rallying it up, and just kind of putting their foot down and saying, 'Enough is enough.' We grew a little bit today."

—HEAD COACH ANDY REID

Kelce kicked up the dirt for 107 receiving yards. Eric Bieniemy made a coaching point to Damien Williams.

GAME 3 | SEPTEMBER 22, 2019, AT ARROWHEAD

THE WINNING EDGE
CHIEFS 33, RAVENS 28

On the traditional festive occasion of the home opener at Arrowhead, fans saw an intermittent rainstorm and a glimpse of pro football's future—the 2018 MVP Patrick Mahomes dueling the player destined to become the 2019 MVP, Lamar Jackson, in a showdown of dynamic young quarterbacks. While Jackson and the resurgent Ravens started strong, the Chiefs' quick-strike capability proved irresistible once again, with two late scores in the first half, and just enough big plays in the second half to hold off a furious Ravens rally and keep the Chiefs unbeaten.

Damien Wilson and Derrick Nnadi stopped Jackson short on the Ravens' early two-point conversion attempt.

"I feel like we kind of let them back into the game. The quarterback made some big-time plays. Kudos to him. They came out of halftime battling. We, as a defense, have to step up and finish them when we have them."

—DEFENSIVE LINEMAN CHRIS JONES, ON THE RAVENS' SECOND-HALF RALLY

McCoy ran for 54 yards and a touchdown.

Arrowhead was festive for the 48th home opener in stadium history.

THE GAME STORY • Leading by five with just under two minutes left, Chiefs' quarterback Patrick Mahomes found tailback Darrel Williams for a 16-yard gain on third-and-nine to seal the victory despite a persistent Ravens' rally, sending the Chiefs faithful home with a win in the home opener.

Mahomes completed 27-of-37 passes for 374 yards and three touchdowns on the day, leading Kansas City back from an early deficit to build a double-digit lead.

Trailing by six after an early Ravens' touchdown drive, the Chiefs scored 23 unanswered points before halftime behind huge performances from tailback LeSean McCoy, wide receiver Mecole Hardman, and tight end Travis Kelce.

McCoy was responsible for the Chiefs' first touchdown of the day—answering the Ravens' score with a 1-yard plunge over the goal line—before wide receiver Demarcus Robinson followed up his two-touchdown performance last week against Oakland with an 18-yard, one-handed scoring grab.

It was then Hardman's turn a drive later, as the rookie hauled in an 83-yard touchdown from Mahomes to make it three-straight drives for Kansas City that ended in touchdowns. Hardman finished the game with a team-leading 97 yards through the air.

The Ravens responded with a score of their own following the break, as tailback Mark Ingram dashed ahead for a 19-yard touchdown to bring Baltimore within 10, but McCoy was back in the end zone on a 14-yard catch late in the third quarter to again extend the Chiefs' lead.

Baltimore went on to narrow the deficit to just three points with 15 fourth-quarter points, but Mahomes found Williams on third down to extend their final drive and secure the win.

Defensively, the Chiefs' held off Ravens' quarterback Lamar Jackson and the league's top statistical offense despite their fourth-quarter rally. Defensive end Emmanuel Ogbah was right in the middle of that performance, tallying three quarterback hurries, 1.5 sacks, and a pass defensed on the afternoon. Fellow defensive end Frank Clark also notched a sack—his first of the 2019 season—while safety Tyrann Mathieu tallied three defensed passes.

—MATT McMULLEN

THE BIG PLAYS

2ND QUARTER, 14:21, BAL 6-0 | CHIEFS BALL, 3RD & GOAL AT BAL 1

After being stuffed twice, the Chiefs run again on a crucial third-down, as LeSean McCoy charges in to give KC the lead.

2ND QUARTER, 3:12, KC 13-6 | CHIEFS BALL, 1ST & 10 AT KC 17

Patrick Mahomes finds rookie speedster Mecole Hardman splitting the secondary on a go route, for an 83-yard touchdown pass that puts the Chiefs up by 14.

4TH QUARTER, 1:51, KC 33-28 | CHIEFS BALL, 3RD & 9 AT KC 37

With the Ravens on the verge of getting the ball back, the Chiefs refuse to play it safe, as Mahomes finds Darrel Williams on a screen pass that gains 16 yards and finishes off the game.

Robinson's second-quarter touchdown catch extended the Chiefs' lead; Jackson and Mahomes exchanged postgame greetings.

"Fans, unbelievable. It was loud and crazy down there. We loved it. The field crew, my hat goes out to the field crew that took care of that field after the torrential downpour that we had. And then I was proud of our guys, particularly our defense for bearing down in the tough times. Fourth down calls, two-point plays, those ended up being big for us."

—HEAD COACH ANDY REID

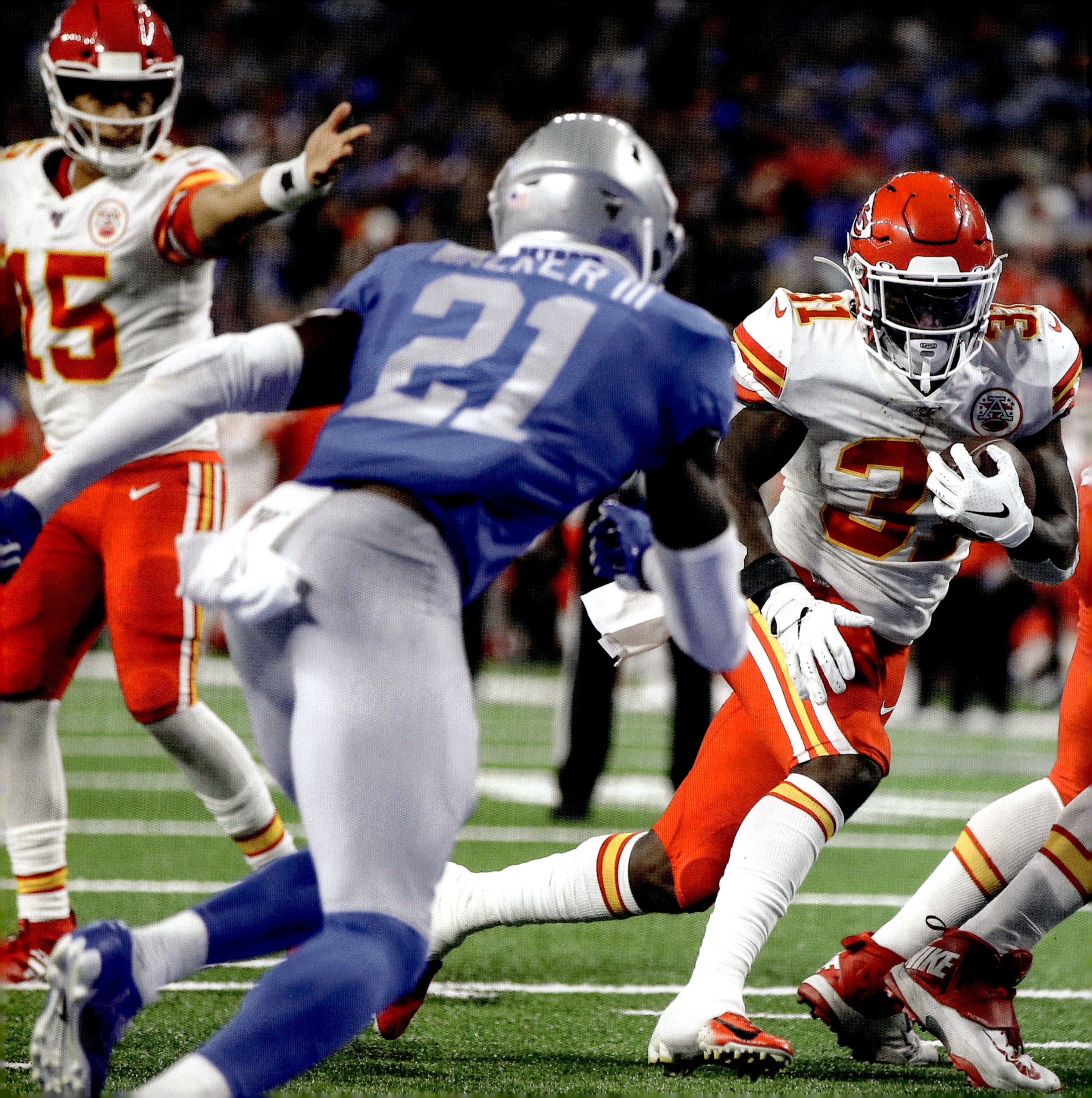
21
31
NIKE

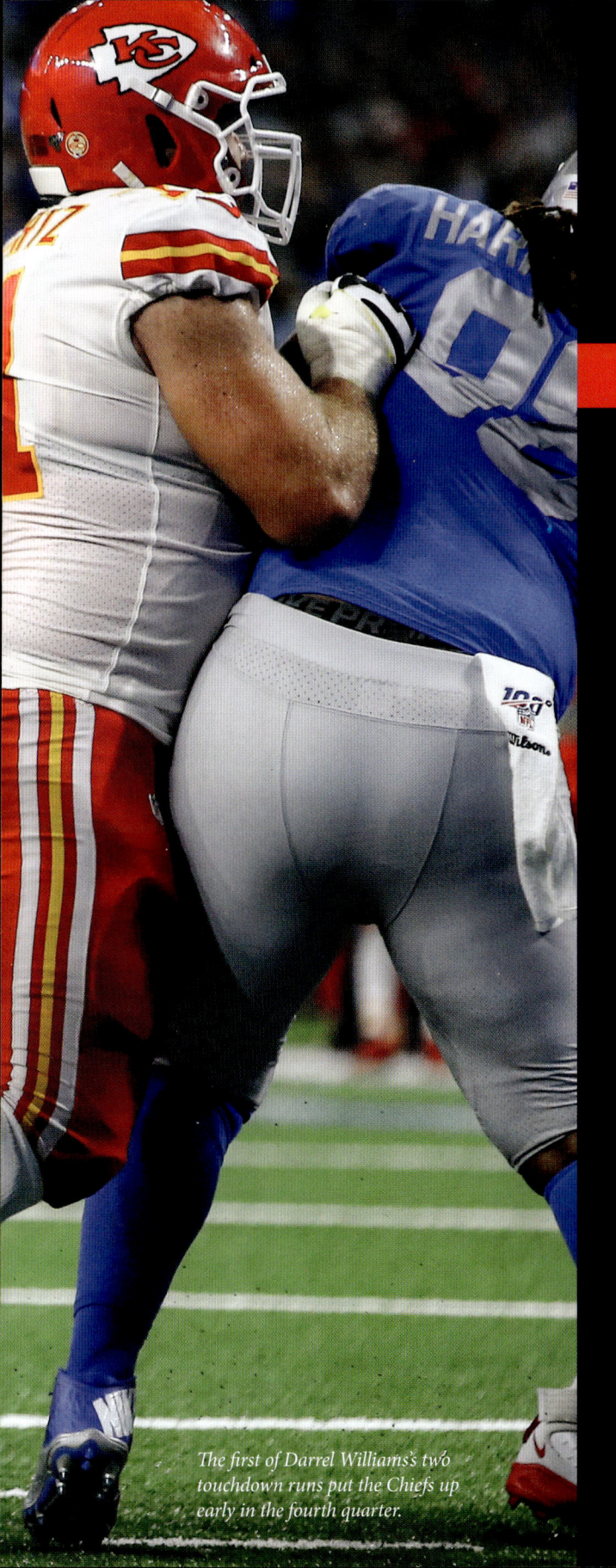

GAME 4 | SEPTEMBER 29, 2019, AT DETROIT

MAGIC IN MOTOWN

CHIEFS 34, LIONS 30

Some football games are orderly and logical, with a conventional rhythm and flow. This one was the other kind: 60 minutes of jitterbugging chaos, five lead changes, a fumble returned 100 yards, and an impromptu hook-and-lateral play. At the end, though, there was time on the clock, a game to be won, and Patrick Mahomes holding the ball—and the sense that somehow, some way, Kansas City would prevail. It took a fourth-down scramble on the final drive, and the game-winning touchdown with just 23 seconds remaining, but the Chiefs stayed unbeaten.

The first of Darrel Williams's two touchdown runs put the Chiefs up early in the fourth quarter.

Pregame scene in the visitors tunnel at Ford Field.

After the Lions' Johnson was stopped near the goal line and lost the ball stretching for a touchdown, the alert Breeland picked up the ball and took it all the way back for a Chiefs score.

THE GAME STORY ▪ After falling behind by three points with just over two minutes left, Chiefs' quarterback Patrick Mahomes led Kansas City on a 13-play, 79-yard drive to retake the lead with just seconds left as tailback Darrel Williams plunged ahead for the go-ahead score.

Mahomes completed 24-of-42 passes for 315 yards in the game, but perhaps his biggest play of the day came on the ground. Facing a fourth-and-eight at midfield on the Chiefs' final drive, Mahomes scrambled for 15 yards to move the chains and set up the eventual score.

The Chiefs fell behind 10–0 for the second straight week, but went on to claw their way back into the contest. Chiefs' tailback LeSean McCoy scored Kansas City's first touchdown, scoring on a 1-yard rush to tie the game up after Detroit's fast start.

The two teams traded field goals after that, setting the stage for a wild third quarter that included five lost fumbles and no shortage of excitement. It began when defensive tackle Derrick Nnadi stripped the ball free from Lions' quarterback Matthew Stafford and fellow defensive lineman Chris Jones recovered, just one play after a Detroit touchdown was overruled by video review.

The Chiefs soon lost a fumble of their own on offense, but after the Lions drove it all the way down to Kansas City's 1-yard line, the defense made another huge play.

Xavier Williams punched the ball free from Lion Kerryon Johnson and cornerback Bashaud Breeland returned it 100 yards for a touchdown, just the fourth 100-yard fumble return for a score in league history.

Detroit scored 10 unanswered points to retake the lead early in the fourth quarter, but the Chiefs responded, with Darrel Williams scoring from close range. But the Lions soon answered back, Stafford hitting wide receiver Kenny Golladay for a 6-yard, go-ahead touchdown with just over two minutes left in regulation.

Mahomes then took the field for Kansas City's final drive, and the rest is history.

—MATT McMULLEN

"I saw it down, I didn't hear no whistle, I saw my teammate pick it up and he kind of put it back down, and I still didn't hear a whistle. So I just went and picked it up and just ran with it, just hoping it wasn't down."

—CORNERBACK BASHAUD BREELAND,
ON HIS 100-YARD FUMBLE RETURN

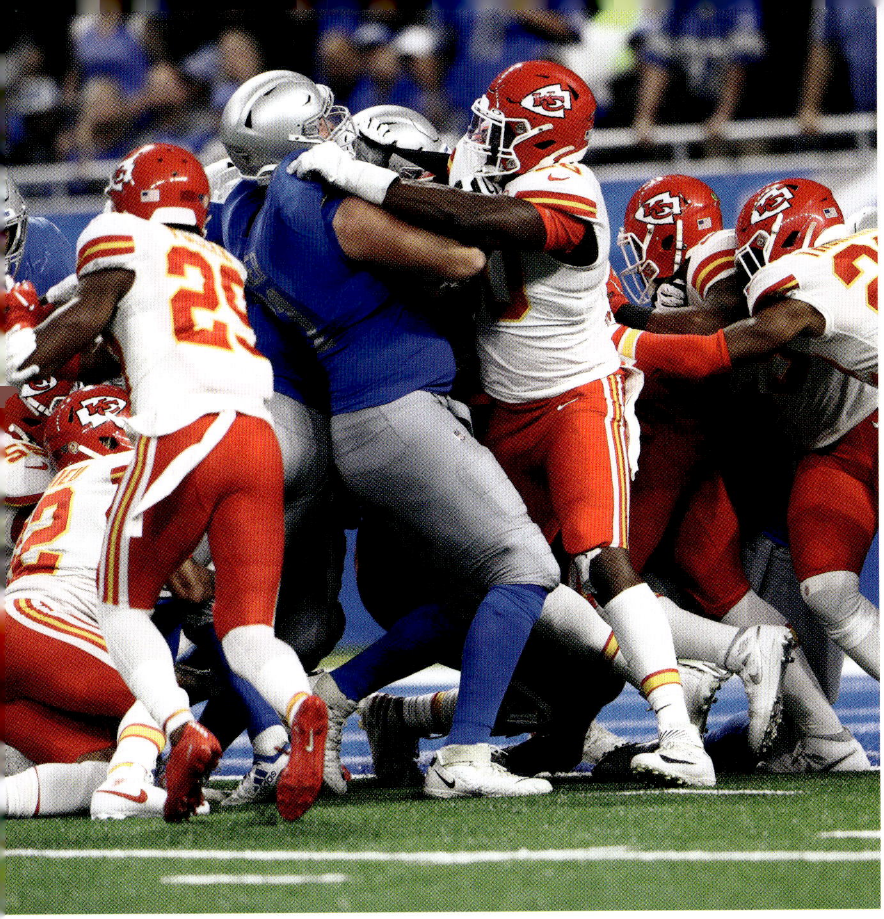

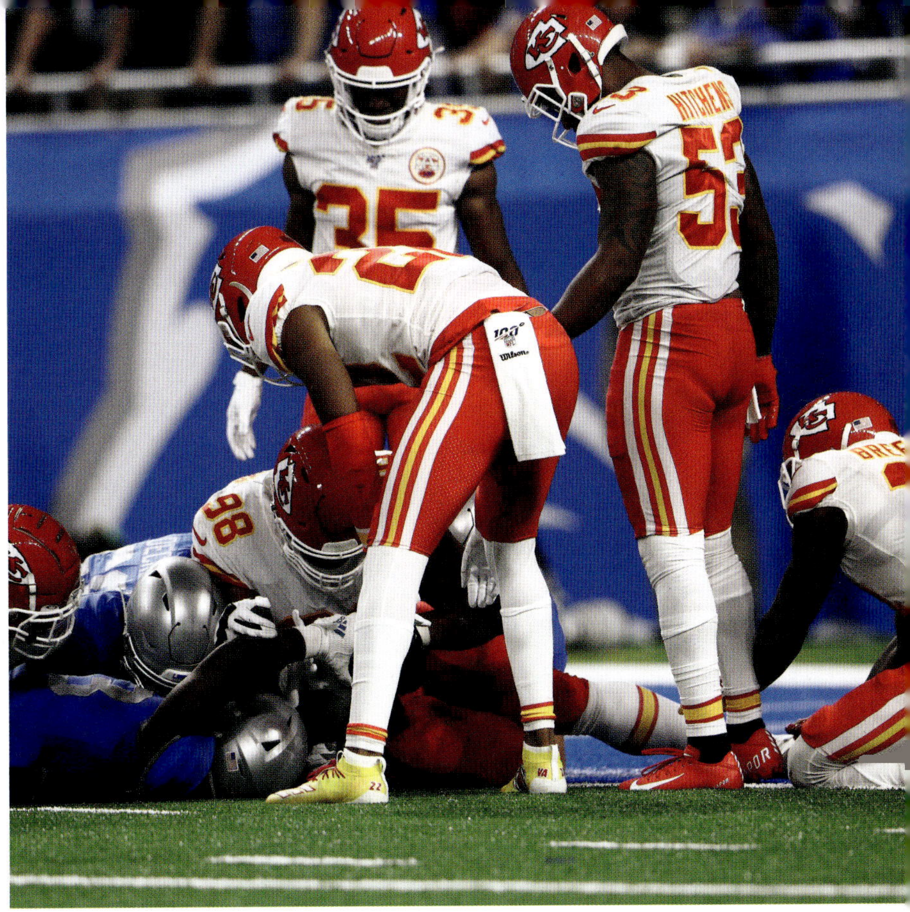
HITCHENS

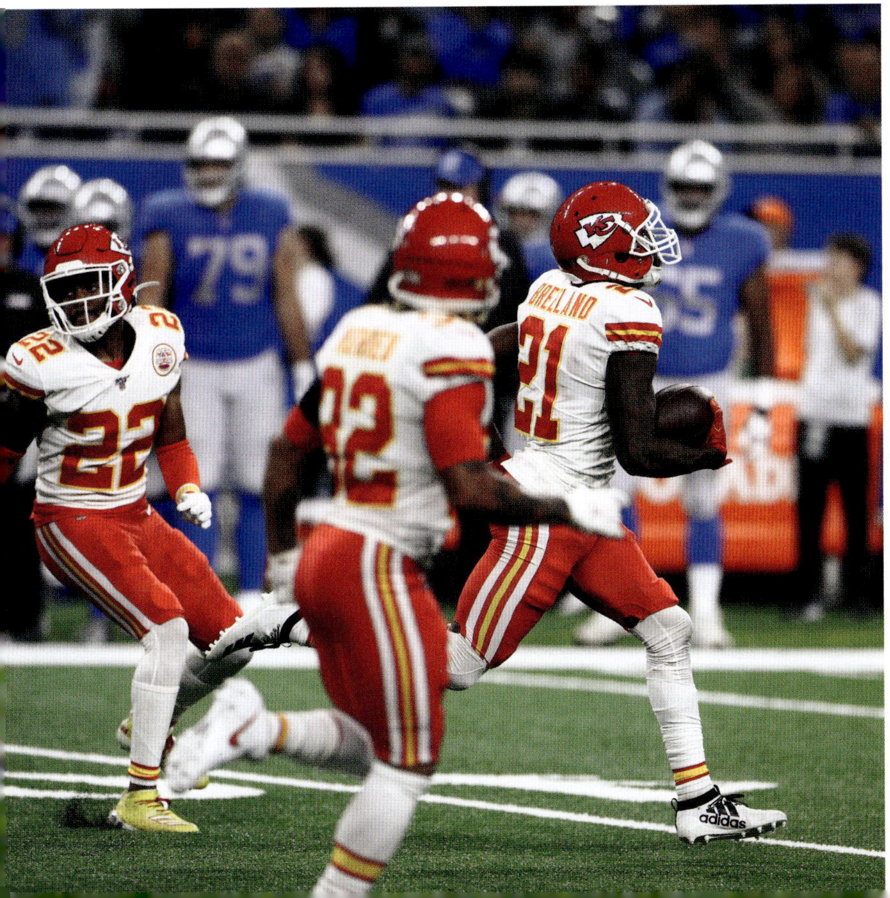
BRELAND

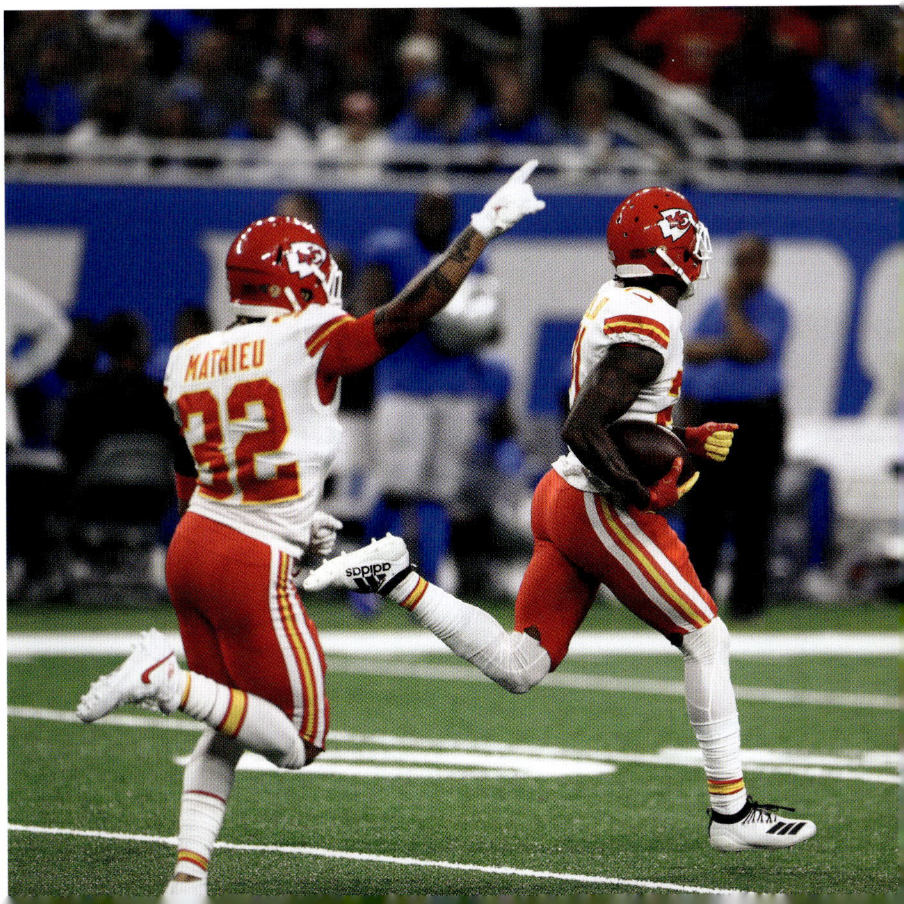
MATHIEU

THE BIG PLAYS

3RD QUARTER, 9:31, 13-13 | LIONS BALL, 3RD & GOAL AT KC 1
After the defense forces a Kerryon Johnson fumble near the goal, Bashaud Breeland picks it up and runs 100 yards for a Chiefs touchdown.

4TH QUARTER, 15:00, DET 23-20 | CHIEFS BALL, 2ND & 12 AT DET 46
Patrick Mahomes scrambles and throws across his body to Travis Kelce at the 34, and he laterals to an onrushing LeSean McCoy who carries it down to the 13.

4TH QUARTER, 1:55, DET 30-27 | CHIEFS BALL, 4TH & 8 AT KC 34
With the game in the balance and his receivers covered, Mahomes takes off and scrambles 15 yards to keep the final drive alive.

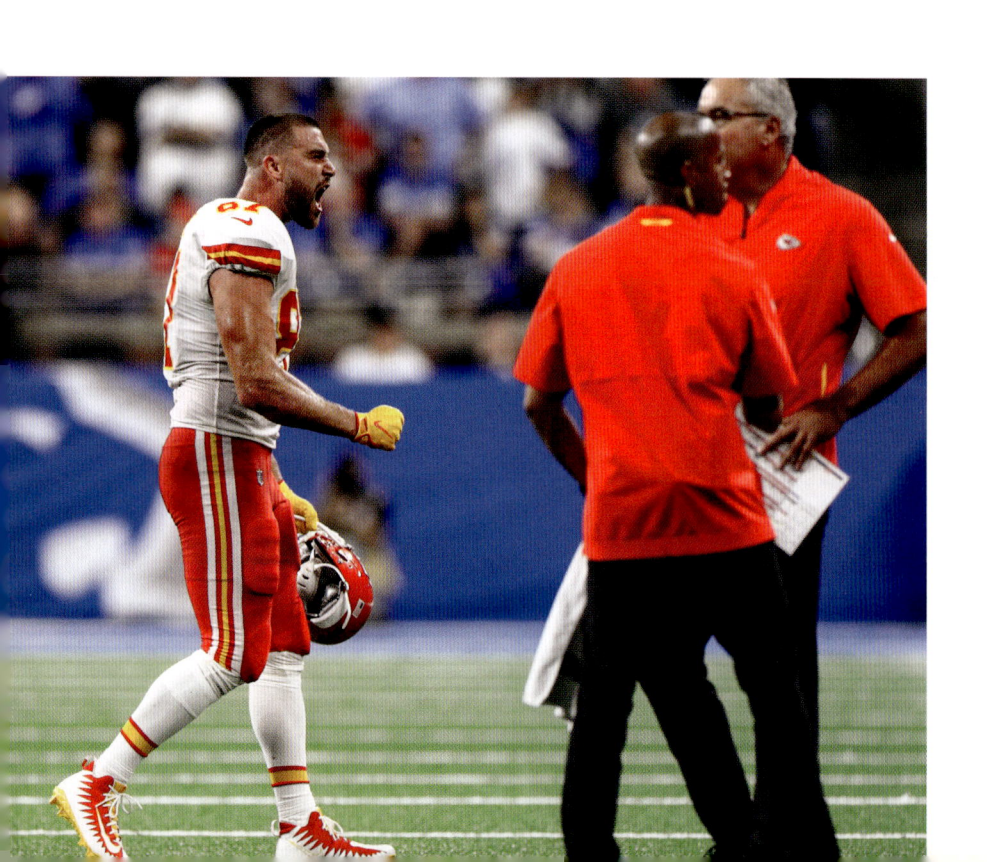

Kelce was fired up with the Chiefs' rally; Laurent Duvernay-Tardif, Anthony Sherman, and Austin Reiter exulted in the locker room after; Tyrann Mathieu sacked the Lions' Stafford late.

"You fight through adversity. In this league, it's not always going to be pretty, it's not always going to be 50 points and three-touchdown wins. So for us, we know that this win—of not playing our best football and finding a way to win—is going to help us tremendously as we get to the end of the season."

—QUARTERBACK PATRICK MAHOMES

GAME 5 | OCTOBER 6, 2019, AT ARROWHEAD

FAILURE TO LAUNCH

COLTS 19, CHIEFS 13

Decked out in all red on a Sunday Night Football center stage, with a national television audience watching, the Chiefs played well in stretches but kept self-destructing at key moments. There were too many penalties, too many sacks, too many turnovers, and a crucial fourth-and-one conversion that came up short. The resourceful Colts, one season after getting blown out in a playoff game at Arrowhead, controlled the ball and the clock, and in the process knocked the Chiefs from the ranks of the undefeated.

Jordan Wilkins was part of a Colts rushing attack that put up 180 yards.

"Obviously, we didn't block. You can have the best quarterback in the world, the best receivers and all that stuff and it just doesn't matter when the guys are getting there too soon. We knew it would be a good challenge for us. Obviously, we didn't live up to expectations."

—OFFENSIVE TACKLE MITCHELL SCHWARTZ

THE GAME STORY · Trailing by six with just over five minutes to play, Chiefs' tailback Damien Williams was stopped on fourth down at Kansas City's 34-yard line. The Colts took over and added a field goal to go up nine points with just two and a half minutes left, sealing the victory.

Chiefs' quarterback Patrick Mahomes completed 22-of-39 passes for 321 yards and a touchdown in the game, tossing a 28-yard scoring strike to wide receiver Byron Pringle on an incredible scramble that featured the reigning league MVP change directions multiple times before firing a dart while on the run.

The play—which came on third-and-18—briefly pushed the Chiefs in front, 10–7, before Indianapolis tied the game with a field goal a drive later. The Colts added another field goal before halftime to re-claim the lead, giving way to a defensive struggle through the final two quarters of play in which both teams combined for just nine points.

Colts' kicker Adam Vinatieri was responsible for six of those points, and while the Chiefs kept it close throughout and narrowed the deficit to just six with just over a minute left, Kansas City never retook the lead.

Pringle put together the best night of his young career in the loss, hauling in six catches for 103 yards and a score.

Rookie wide receiver Mecole Hardman also had a strong night, tallying four catches for 79 yards.

Defensively, safety Tyrann Mathieu tallied his first interception as a member of the Chiefs while linebacker Damien Wilson led all players with 12 tackles.

But it was an unusually disappointing night for the Chiefs' offense, which saw its record streak of 22 straight games scoring at least 26 points come to an end. That was due in part to the Colts strong running game—Marlon Mack led the way with 29 carries for 132 yards—but also 11 Chiefs penalties, for 125 yards.

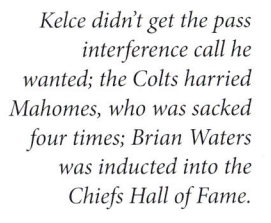

—MATT McMULLEN

Kelce didn't get the pass interference call he wanted; the Colts harried Mahomes, who was sacked four times; Brian Waters was inducted into the Chiefs Hall of Fame.

GAME 6 | OCTOBER 13, 2019, AT ARROWHEAD

GROUND DOWN

TEXANS 31, CHIEFS 24

There were moments of brilliance—the defense stopping two drives with interceptions in the end zone, a pair of terrific touchdown catches for the returning Tyreek Hill—but for the second week in a row, there were also too many mistakes to win a football game against a good team. A Patrick Mahomes fumble late in the first half hurt, as did an atypical dropped pass by Hill in a key third-down situation. But the final analysis was as old as football itself: If you can't stop the run, you can't win the game.

Hyde, traded by the Chiefs in the preseason, came back with 116 yards and a touchdown.

"You have to reboot. We have to get back to our aggression, our passion for stopping the run. Early in the season, we have not been able to do that. That's just being honest. Over 100 yards rushing every week against our opponents, some running backs are more well-known than others, but we are making everybody look awesome."

—DEFENSIVE END FRANK CLARK

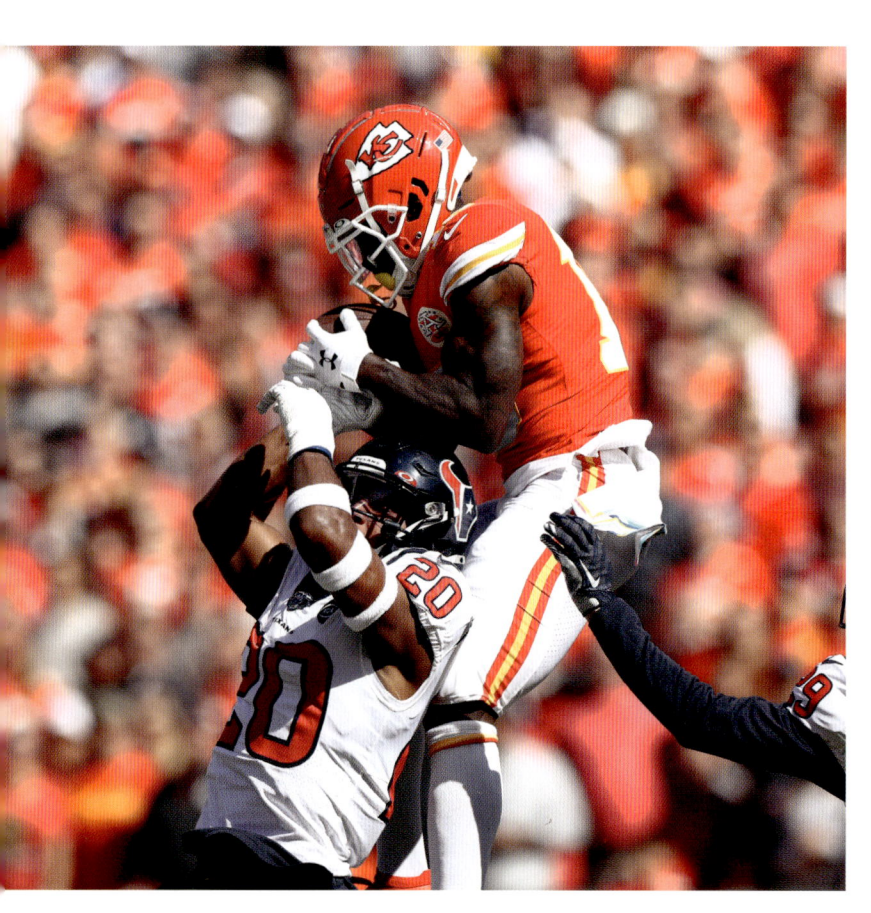

Clockwise from above: Hill returned to action with two touchdown catches; Juan Thornhill made a key end zone interception; Tyrann Mathieu congratulated former teammate Watson in the waning seconds.

THE GAME STORY · Leading by a touchdown with just over two minutes to go deep in Chiefs' territory, Texans' quarterback Deshaun Watson found wide receiver DeAndre Hopkins on fourth-and-three to move the chains and seal the victory for Houston. It marked the end of a back-and-forth game that saw momentum swing both ways.

Chiefs' quarterback Patrick Mahomes completed 19-of-35 passes for 273 yards and three touchdowns in the contest, finding wide receiver Tyreek Hill for a 46-yard score on Kansas City's opening drive.

Facing a third-and-21, Mahomes fired the ball downfield to connect with the leaping Hill, who then fell into the end zone for his first touchdown of the season. Hill hauled in five catches for 80 yards and two touchdowns in his first game-action since Week 1.

On Houston's first play from scrimmage following Hill's score, defensive end Frank Clark jarred the ball loose from tailback Carlos Hyde before recovering it deep in Texans' territory. The Chiefs turned the takeaway into a field goal, and got back in the end zone a drive later as Mahomes found Damien Williams on a 14-yard score to extend the lead.

But the 17–3 lead wouldn't last, on a day where Houston gashed the Chiefs for 192 yards rushing, taking a 20–17 halftime lead.

Houston appeared to be on the verge of adding to that lead on their opening drive of the third quarter, but a huge tackle by safety Daniel Sorensen on third down followed by a missed field goal kept the score within six. The Chiefs then took advantage, as Mahomes found Hill for a 6-yard, go-ahead touchdown on Kansas City's next possession.

Later, cornerback Charvarius Ward picked off Watson in the end zone to hold the Texans without points on a second-straight long drive.

Watson cashed in a drive later, however, leading Houston on a 12-play, 93-yard drive to reclaim the lead.

The Chiefs couldn't get much going on the following possession, and after Watson's fourth-down conversion, Mahomes and company didn't have another chance to tie things up.

—MATT McMULLEN

Mahomes's dislocated kneecap put his immediate future—and the season—in doubt.

GAME 7 | OCTOBER 17, 2019, AT DENVER

MILE HIGH ANXIETY

CHIEFS 30, BRONCOS 6

In the moments after the play—as the pile-up near the goal line pointedly did not unpile, and it became clear that the man at the bottom was No. 15—a hush fell over both the stadium and Chiefs Kingdom. But after Patrick Mahomes limped off the field under his own power, the Chiefs rallied around their injured leader (as well as the next man up, Matt Moore) and stifled the Broncos offense, rolling to yet another convincing division victory in their best defensive performance of the young season.

Hitchens's strip-sack of Flacco led to a Ragland fumble recovery and a Chiefs touchdown.

THE GAME STORY · The Chiefs lost quarterback Patrick Mahomes to a knee injury early in the second quarter, but veteran quarterback Matt Moore and a tenacious effort by the defense helped Kansas City snap its two-game losing streak, and secure an eighth-straight victory over the rival Broncos.

Moore completed 10-of-19 passes for 117 yards and a touchdown in relief of Mahomes, tossing a 57-yard scoring strike to wide receiver Tyreek Hill midway through the third quarter. It marked the 17th touchdown of Hill's career that covered 50+ yards in just 50 games as a professional.

Fellow receiver Mecole Hardman also found the end zone in the contest, hauling in a 21-yard touchdown pass from Mahomes early in the game before the reigning league MVP departed.

Defensively, the Chiefs pass rush collected nine sacks on the night, wreaking havoc on Broncos' quarterback Joe Flacco throughout the game.

After the Broncos tallied a touchdown on their opening possession, the Chiefs held Denver out of the end zone and to just 130 yards of total offense. Additionally, the Broncos converted just one of 13 third-down attempts on the evening.

Linebackers Anthony Hitchens and Reggie Ragland turned one of those sacks into six points, as Hitchens stripped the ball free from Flacco before Ragland scooped it up and dashed ahead 5 yards for the first touchdown of his career.

That all proved to be enough against Denver as Kansas City scored 30 unanswered points following the Broncos' opening score to move to 5-2 on the campaign.

—MATT McMULLEN

"You've seen that over the years where teams let themselves down when one of your best players gets hurt, particularly the quarterback. But I was proud of how our guys stepped up and just kept battling."

—HEAD COACH ANDY REID

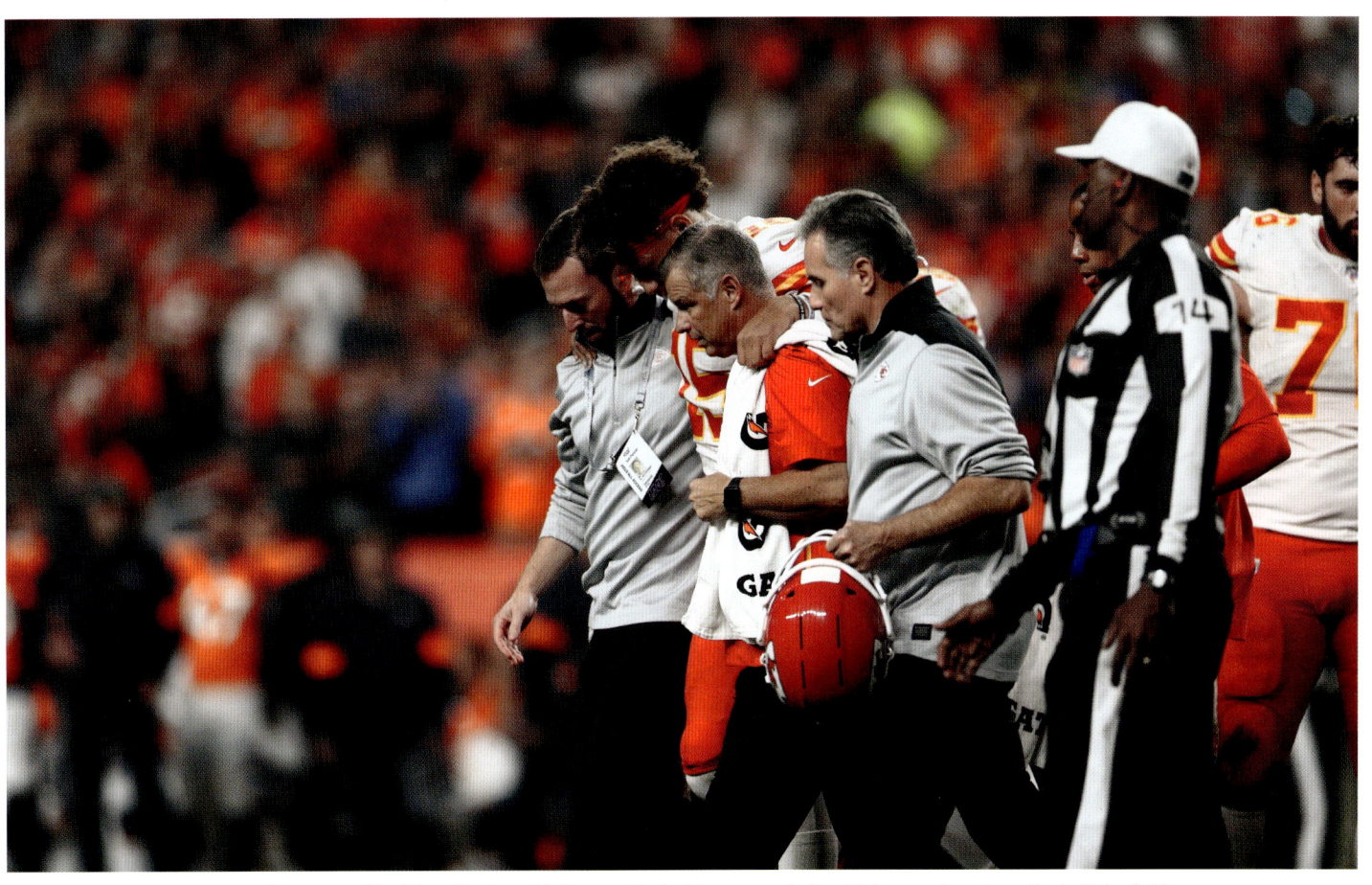

Laurent Duvernay-Tardif and LeSean McCoy watched with concern before Mahomes gingerly walked off the field.

By the end of the game, Chiefs fans had taken over the lower bowl in Denver.

"When the MVP goes down, everybody has to step up. We did that. Matt came in and did a great job. We have trust in him. We just had to go out there and play and keep everything the same. We still had a game to win."

—WIDE RECEIVER MECOLE HARDMAN

Steve Spagnuolo's defense excelled.

THE BIG PLAYS

1ST QUARTER, 4:19, DEN 6-0 | CHIEFS BALL, 3RD & 2 AT DEN 21
Patrick Mahomes finds Mecole Hardman on a crossing route, and after bobbling the ball, Hardman evades a defender and sprints in for a touchdown.

2ND QUARTER, 15:00, KC 10-6 | BRONCOS BALL, 4TH & 4 AT DEN 46
A fake-punt attempt by Denver punter Colby Wadman is sniffed out by Armani Watts, who tackles Wadman for a 7-yard loss.

2ND QUARTER, 7:17, KC 13-6 | BRONCOS BALL, 2ND & 9 AT DEN 26
Anthony Hitchens breaks through on a blitz, chops the ball out of Joe Flacco's hand, and Reggie Ragland recovers the fumble and brings it in for a touchdown.

Frank Clark and Travis Kelce celebrated the big road win.

GAME 8 | OCTOBER 27, 2019, AT ARROWHEAD

NARROW MARGINS

PACKERS 31, CHIEFS 24

Kansas City's Matt Moore—who'd been coaching high school football as recently as August—acquitted himself well, filling in for the injured Patrick Mahomes during the game. But the Chiefs were reminded, in a free-wheeling Sunday Night Football matchup, just how special a special quarterback can be. The Packers' irrepressible Aaron Rodgers proved the difference on the night, especially with one seeing-eye touchdown pass thrown while he was being tackled, and the Chiefs fell to their third loss in four games.

Rodgers was a step ahead most of the night, but he couldn't elude a diving Khalen Saunders on this scramble.

"We didn't get the job done. Pretty much played well throughout the whole game. They made some plays. Aaron Rodgers was being Aaron Rodgers. He is going to make those plays. Got another big game next week. That's the NFL."

—SAFETY TYRANN MATHIEU

Moore, making his first start for the Chiefs, threw for 267 yards.

THE GAME STORY · Leading by a touchdown and facing a third-and-five with two minutes remaining, Packers' quarterback Aaron Rodgers found tailback Aaron Jones for a gain of eight to move the chains. The play essentially sealed the victory for the Packers, and while the Chiefs fought hard throughout, Kansas City was ultimately dealt their third loss of the season.

Green Bay jumped out to a 14-point lead in the first quarter, as Rodgers tossed a 4-yard touchdown to Jones before fellow running back Jamaal Williams plowed ahead for a 1-yard score two drives later.

The Chiefs responded with a pair of touchdowns themselves, however, as quarterback Matt Moore tossed scoring strikes to tight end Travis Kelce and wide receiver Mecole Hardman to even the score midway through the second quarter.

Moore found Kelce amid incoming pressure from the Packers' pass-rush, throwing a floater that the All-Pro tight end hauled in for a 29-yard touchdown to get Kansas City on the board.

It marked the 450th catch of Kelce's career, and at just 88 games, the 30-year-old Kelce became the fastest tight end ever to reach the mark.

Following Kelce's score, Hardman then handled a quick toss from Moore on a sweep before darting past and weaving around defenders for a 30-yard score.

The Chiefs completed the early rally as kicker Harrison Butker connected on a 28-yard field goal a drive later, putting Kansas City in front for the first time all night.

The Packers answered with 10 unanswered points of their own to begin the second half, taking a seven-point lead early in the fourth quarter, but Kansas City responded with a 10-play, 75-yard touchdown drive that culminated in a 3-yard scoring dash by tailback Damien Williams.

Green Bay then responded in short order, however, as Rodgers fired a short pass to Jones, who turned upfield and avoided would-be tacklers for a 67-yard, go-ahead score.

The Chiefs couldn't move the chains on their next possession, and they wouldn't possess the ball offensively again as Green Bay ran out the clock.

—MATT McMULLEN

An injured Chris Jones rallied his teammates before the game; Chief greats Johnny Robinson and Tony Gonzalez received their Pro Football Hall of Fame rings in a halftime ceremony.

GAME 9 | NOVEMBER 3, 2019, AT ARROWHEAD

ALIVE AND KICKING
CHIEFS 26, VIKINGS 23

With their starting quarterback out for at least one more week and yet another playoff-caliber team visiting, the Chiefs needed a victory by any means necessary. They did it with defensive grit and by forcing a crucial late three-and-out, moments of brilliance and resilience on offense, and a tense last-minute drive featuring huge catches from Travis Kelce and Tyreek Hill. That culminated in Harrison Butker's game-winning field goal, prompting a celebration that even Patrick Mahomes took part in, though very carefully.

Damien Williams broke away from the Vikings for a 91-yard touchdown run.

"This is an emotional game. The emotions were all over the place today, but to see the team and the guys win at home and rally through all three phases was great to be a part of, and great to see."

—QUARTERBACK MATT MOORE

Clark Hunt and Brett Veach conferred on the field before the game; Hill extended for this early touchdown catch; Chris Jones returned to action with a sack in the big win.

THE GAME STORY · Tied at 23 points apiece, Chiefs' quarterback Matt Moore led Kansas City on a five-play, 19-yard drive in the game's closing seconds to set up Harrison Butker's game-winning 44-yard field goal as time expired, ending a back-and-forth game as Kansas City moved to 6-3 on the year.

Moore finished with 275 passing yards and a touchdown, leading the Chiefs to his first victory as a starting quarterback on the campaign.

Both teams were locked in a defensive battle early, combining for just 20 points through the first half. The Chiefs scored first, as Moore slung a 40-yard scoring strike to wide receiver Tyreek Hill, who reached out to grab his fourth touchdown of the season, part of a season-high 140-yard performance.

The Vikings responded with a scoring drive of their own a possession later, marching 75 yards on 12 plays as quarterback Kirk Cousins found wide receiver Bisi Johnson for a 4-yard touchdown to tie it.

Each team tallied a field goal prior to halftime, before Cousins connected with tailback Ameer Abdullah on a 16-yard touchdown to push Minnesota ahead early in the third quarter.

The Vikings missed the extra point on that touchdown, however, which allowed the Chiefs to retake the lead following a 91-yard touchdown scamper by tailback Damien Williams. His scoring run tied Chiefs' legend Jamaal Charles for the longest touchdown rush in franchise history and marked the longest by any player in the 2019 NFL season.

Minnesota took the lead again early in the fourth quarter, as Cousins found tight end Kyle Rudolph on a 3-yard score, but Kansas City wasn't done. Moore found Hill for multiple gains of double-digit yardage two drives later, setting up a 54-yard, game-tying field goal by Butker with just over two minutes left. It matched the longest field goal of Butker's young career.

The Chiefs' defense didn't allow the Vikings to get anything going on their next possession, setting up Kansas City's final drive and Butker's game-winner.

—MATT McMULLEN

Chiefs defenders circled up prior to the game.

THE BIG PLAYS

1ST QUARTER, 8:28, 0-0 | CHIEFS BALL, 2ND & 10 AT MIN 40
After a play-action fake, Matt Moore lofts the ball down the right sideline and Tyreek Hill extends to make the catch and tumble into the end zone.

3RD QUARTER, 6:25, MIN 16-10 | CHIEFS BALL, 2ND & 4 AT KC 9
Damien Williams finds a crease in the middle, jukes out one defender and outraces everyone else (except Tyreek Hill) on a record-tying 91-yard touchdown run.

4TH QUARTER, 2:36, MIN 23-20 | CHIEFS BALL, 4TH & 27 AT MIN 36
After a 15-yard sack on third down puts the Chiefs nearly out of field goal range, Harrison Butker ties the game with a career-best 54-yard kick.

"*I was jacked up. I was enjoying it in the moment. But to be successful as a kicker, you can't go into a kick with a lot of adrenaline. So, I was just kind of pacing on the sideline, taking deep breaths, trying to get back into that calm mode that I think I do my best at as a kicker.*"

—KICKER HARRISON BUTKER, ON HIS EMOTIONS BETWEEN THE GAME-TYING AND GAME-WINNING FIELD GOALS

Butker's field goal prompted a celebration in which even the injured Mahomes joined in.

Though the Chiefs defense recorded four sacks on the day, Tannehill still engineered the Titans' game-winning drive.

GAME 10 | NOVEMBER 10, 2019, AT TENNESSEE

AGONY OF DEFEAT

TITANS 35, CHIEFS 32

Some losses are more painful than others. Kansas City's narrow defeat to the Titans was particularly galling, in part because it was a game the Chiefs were convinced they'd already won. Patrick Mahomes returned to action and was his usual spectacular self, but there were special teams miscues, an inability to convert on a crucial third-and-short, and a spate of costly penalties. When the game was over, and the Chiefs' division lead was down to a half game, the season had clearly reached a crossroads.

THE GAME STORY · Trailing by five with less than 30 seconds remaining, Titans' quarterback Ryan Tannehill found wide receiver Adam Humphries for a 23-yard touchdown to push Tennessee ahead. The Chiefs moved into field goal range on their following possession, but the 52-yard attempt was blocked as time expired.

It was a frustrating loss, as the usually reliable Chiefs' field goal unit had another attempt foiled by a miscommunication on the snap just minutes earlier. The defeat spoiled a strong outing by quarterback Patrick Mahomes in his return to action, as the reigning league MVP completed 36-of-50 passes for 446 yards and three touchdowns in his first start since Week 7.

After the Chiefs went up 10–0, the Titans responded with 13 unanswered points of their own to claim the lead as linebacker Rashaan Evans scooped up a fumble and returned it 53 yards for a go-ahead touchdown.

Kansas City was back in front midway through the third quarter, as Mahomes found wide receiver Tyreek Hill for an 11-yard touchdown.

Tennessee regained the lead on their next drive, however, when tailback Derrick Henry broke free for a 68-yard touchdown, but the Chiefs quickly jumped back in front when Butker nailed a 43-yard field goal near the end of the third quarter.

The Chiefs extended their advantage a drive later, as Mahomes eluded tacklers and leapt in the air while firing a dart to wide receiver Mecole Hardman, who turned on the burners for an electric 63-yard touchdown.

The Titans then answered with a 10-play, 75-yard touchdown drive of their own to narrow the deficit, as Henry tallied his second score of the day, before Butker connected on a 39-yard field goal to put the Chiefs up by five with just over three minutes left.

Tennessee turned the ball over on downs on their ensuing possession, but the Chiefs weren't able to gain a first down, or convert the field goal attempt, allowing the Titans the final drive that won the game for Tennessee.

—MATT McMULLEN

Hardman's 63-yard touchdown reception put the Chiefs up by nine in the fourth quarter.

Hill celebrated his third-quarter touchdown with a group of Chiefs fans.

NFL rushing leader Henry carried for 188 yards.

"Everybody in this building has played football for a long time, and of course everyone has played a game like that with lots of momentum swings. You think you have it, then you lose it. But that's just the name of the game. It really hurts. Everyone's feeling that right now."

—GUARD ANDREW WYLIE, ON LOSING THE LATE LEAD

GAME 11 | NOVEMBER 18, 2019, AT MEXICO CITY

¡VAMOS, CHIEFS!
CHIEFS 24, CHARGERS 17

With the eyes of two nations on Mexico City, the Chiefs and Chargers met at the historic Estadio Azteca—site of two World Cup finals—for a crucial Monday Night Football game. Though the venue was different, the result was the same, as the Chiefs continued their recent mastery over the Chargers in another road victory featuring lots of red in the stands. The rebuilt Chiefs' defense made big plays, with four interceptions of the Chargers' Philip Rivers, including Daniel Sorensen's late game-clincher in the end zone.

Mike Pennel set the tone with a first-quarter sack of Rivers.

"At the end of the day we don't mind being in those kind of football games. I felt like we have been challenged a lot this season. We played a lot of good football teams, a lot of good quarterbacks. And so I think our defense is starting to get confidence. I think we're starting to want to be in that situation, so we can make a play and we can get the ball back to our offense."

—SAFETY TYRANN MATHIEU

Mahomes congratulated Kelce after his third-quarter touchdown; Sorensen celebrated after his game-clinching interception; Mathieu's key second-quarter interception set up the Chiefs' first touchdown.

THE GAME STORY · Leading by seven points with just 24 seconds left, Chiefs' safety Daniel Sorensen picked off Chargers' quarterback Philip Rivers in the end zone to seal the victory for Kansas City.

Chiefs' quarterback Patrick Mahomes completed 19-of-32 passes for 182 yards and a touchdown, finding tight end Travis Kelce seven times for 92 yards.

The Chargers took an early lead with a field goal, before Rivers tossed interceptions on back-to-back drives midway through the first half. The first came when defensive end Frank Clark tore the ball from Rivers's hand, and it fell into the arms of defensive tackle Derrick Nnadi. Safety Tyrann Mathieu was responsible for Rivers's second turnover, sprinting across the field to snatch the ball before returning it 35 yards down to the Chargers' 6-yard line.

Chiefs' tailback LeSean McCoy then cashed in on the takeaway a snap later, plunging ahead for a 6-yard touchdown to put Kansas City in front.

Kansas City opened the second half with a 75-yard touchdown drive, as tailback Darrel Williams ran it over from 6 yards to extend the Chiefs' lead to 17–9.

The Chiefs' defense held Los Angeles without a first down on their ensuing drive, and just five minutes later, Mahomes had Kansas City back on the scoreboard with a 23-yard scoring strike to Kelce.

Los Angeles answered, however, when Rivers hit wide receiver Keenan Allen on a 7-yard touchdown, and following a successful two-point try, the margin was back to just seven points.

The two teams then traded possessions without yielding a single point, with Clark making drive-stalling plays on consecutive defensive series before rookie cornerback Rashad Fenton picked off Rivers late in the fourth quarter.

Los Angeles had one final chance with just under two minutes remaining and moved into the red zone as Rivers hit wide receiver Mike Williams on a 50-yard pass in the final seconds. But Sorensen nabbed the ball out of the air four plays later to preserve the lead.

—MATT McMULLEN

The façade of Estadio Azteca, hours before kickoff.

THE BIG PLAYS

2ND QUARTER, 13:34, LAC 3-0 | CHARGERS BALL, 2ND & 9 AT KC 25
Frank Clark hits Philip Rivers as he's about to pass, and the ball sails in the air, caught by Derrick Nnadi for an interception.

2ND QUARTER, 9:01, LAC 3-0 | CHARGERS BALL, 3RD & 8 AT LAC 27
Tyrann Mathieu sprints in front of Keenan Allen to intercept Philip Rivers, returning the ball 35 yards to the Chargers 6, to set up the Chiefs' first touchdown.

4TH QUARTER, 0:24, KC 24-17 | CHARGERS BALL, 2ND & 10 AT KC 14
With the game on the line, Rivers lofts the ball toward Austin Ekeler in the corner of the end zone, but Daniel Sorensen leaps to intercept and seals the win.

"It was amazing, honestly. The stadium, when you get to walk out that tunnel and see the stadium, how big, and you can just tell the history in it. So to be a part of that is awesome. And then the fans were amazing. They were cheering the whole game. It was loud; it was a great atmosphere."

—QUARTERBACK PATRICK MAHOMES

Chiefs Kingdom was well represented in Mexico City; Andy Reid and Kelce exulted in the key divisional victory.

When Mahomes scrambled in from 13 yards in the second quarter, the rout was on.

GAME 12 | DECEMBER 1, 2019, AT ARROWHEAD

WESTERN STARS

CHIEFS 40, RAIDERS 9

The best teams start playing their best football by December. So it was in Kansas City; after grinding out tight wins over the Vikings and the Chargers in recent weeks, the Chiefs dispatched the Oakland Raiders with emphatic ease, reasserting their dominance of the AFC West. While the offense was fine, it was the defense that again rose up, forcing two key turnovers in the first half: Tyrann Mathieu's first-quarter interception set up the Chiefs' first touchdown, and rookie Juan Thornhill's pick-six gave the Chiefs a 21–0 second-quarter lead. From there, they cruised.

THE GAME STORY · The Chiefs' dominant performances in all three phases led to an impressive win—their 25th in the last 28 divisional contests—and maintained Kansas City's grip on first place in the AFC West, securing the tiebreaker over Oakland with another season sweep of their storied rival. In a sign of how disciplined and dominant the performance was, the Chiefs didn't commit a single penalty on the day.

Chiefs' quarterback Patrick Mahomes completed 15-of-29 passes for 175 yards and a touchdown in the game, finding tailback Darrel Williams for a 3-yard touchdown on Kansas City's opening possession.

Mahomes also managed to find the end zone with his legs a bit later—scrambling for a 13-yard score midway through the second quarter to extend Kansas City's advantage—before safety Juan Thornhill picked off Raiders' quarterback Derek Carr a possession later and brought it all the way back for a 46-yard pick-six.

Thornhill's interception was one of three takeaways for Kansas City on the afternoon, including an interception by fellow safety Tyrann Mathieu that set up Williams's score early in the game.

Kansas City later built on its lead when tailback LeSean McCoy rushed ahead for a 3-yard touchdown, pushing the Chiefs ahead by 31 and effectively putting the contest out of reach. Rookie tailback Darwin Thompson also found the end zone late in the game, plunging ahead for a 3-yard touchdown.

Chiefs' tight end Travis Kelce led all pass-catchers with 90 yards through the air while defensive linemen Chris Jones and Tanoh Kpassagnon each recorded a sack. The defense—which held Oakland scoreless until early in the fourth quarter—tallied its first shutout through three quarters of action since doing so last season, also against the Raiders at Arrowhead.

—MATT McMULLEN

The Legion of Zoom—Tyreek Hill, Sammy Watkins, Mecole Hardman, Demarcus Robinson, Gehrig Dieter, and Byron Pringle—gathered pregame; Jones harried the Raiders' Derek Carr all day; Thornhill tackled the Raiders' Trevor Davis short of the marker on a fourth-down play, then later scored on a Pick Six.

"It was a blast out there! To see the defense, especially, go out and have a game like that, it really brings the offense to life. We were moving the ball and making plays, too. Overall, it was just a great team win—this feels great."

—GUARD ANDREW WYLIE

Teammates circled Jones prior to the start of the game. Ward's Pick Two on the Raiders' late conversion attempt gave the Chiefs their final points.

"It started when Pat went out. We put higher expectations on ourselves, because we knew we had to do more with him being out. And now that he's back, I think we just capitalized on that momentum."

—DEFENSIVE END ALEX OKAFOR,
ON THE IMPROVED DEFENSE

THE BIG PLAYS

2ND QUARTER, 9:58, KC 7–0 | RAIDERS BALL, 4TH & 1 AT OAK 40
With the Raiders going for it on fourth down in their own territory, Juan Thornhill tackles Trevor Davis for no gain on a jet sweep, giving the Chiefs offense a short field.

2ND QUARTER, 6:37, KC 7–0 | CHIEFS BALL, 1ST & 10 AT OAK 13
Patrick Mahomes takes the shotgun snap and, finding his receivers covered, scrambles to his left and beats the Raiders to the pylon for a touchdown.

2ND QUARTER, 3:52, KC 14–0 | RAIDERS BALL, 2ND & 8 AT OAK 40
Thornhill intercepts a Derek Carr pass intended for Tyrell Williams and returns it 46 yards for a pick-six.

Mathieu, after another interception, accepted fans' congratulations postgame.

GAME 13 | DECEMBER 8, 2019, AT NEW ENGLAND

POWER SHIFT

CHIEFS 23, PATRIOTS 16

For the better part of two decades, the balance of power in the AFC resided in New England. But with a gritty, dedicated performance, the Chiefs served notice that they could go anywhere and beat anyone. In a tense game, they survived a late rally, with Bashaud Breeland knocking away Tom Brady's fourth-down pass in the end zone. The team flew home satisfied with a division title, a statement victory, a tiebreaker advantage that might prove crucial later, and new shirts that said it all: THE WEST IS NOT ENOUGH.

Frank Clark's sack of Brady thwarted a second-quarter drive.

"You want to play against the best. These are the reigning world champions. If you're going to do that, then you better be mentally prepared to play for four quarters. I thought the guys did that. I mean, that's what ended up happening and I'm proud of them for that."

—HEAD COACH ANDY REID

THE GAME STORY · The Chiefs outlasted a late Patriots' rally to secure the victory and—coupled with the Oakland Raiders' loss—lock up a fourth-straight AFC West title in the process. After yielding a touchdown on New England's opening drive, Kansas City went on to score 23 unanswered points to build a sizable lead before the Patriots pulled within a single score early in the fourth quarter.

New England quarterback Tom Brady then led the Patriots all the way to Kansas City's 5-yard line with just over a minute left in regulation, but Chiefs' cornerback Bashaud Breeland batted Brady's pass incomplete on fourth down to preserve the victory.

Chiefs' quarterback Patrick Mahomes completed 26-of-40 passes for 283 yards and a touchdown in the game, connecting with wide receiver Mecole Hardman on a 48-yard score to push Kansas City in front early in the second quarter.

Breeland then picked off Brady a snap later, setting up a 4-yard rushing touchdown by tight end Travis Kelce—who took the direct snap out of the wildcat formation—to push the Chiefs ahead by double-digits.

The defense managed to generate pressure on Brady and the Patriots' offense throughout the game. Kansas City's pass rush tallied six hits and three sacks on Brady, holding the Patriots to just seven points until late in the third quarter.

New England rallied to bring the score within 10 points, however, as tailback Brandon Bolden found the end zone on a 10-yard rush following a blocked punt a few plays earlier. The Patriots later narrowed the deficit to seven points with a fourth-quarter field goal.

The two teams then traded possessions before Kansas City punted it away to New England with just over five minutes left, but the Chiefs' defense ultimately held in the shadow of their own goal post to lock up the victory.

At 24 years old, Mahomes became the youngest quarterback in the Brady-Bill Belichick era to defeat New England on the road in the regular season, snapping New England's 21-game home win streak.

—MATT McMULLEN

Tanoh Kpassagnon's blocked field goal attempt keyed an important first-half stop; Kelce scored a key rushing touchdown on a direct snap; Breeland's last-minute pass deflection clinched the game for the Chiefs.

THE BIG PLAYS

2ND QUARTER, 13:14, NE 7-3 | CHIEFS BALL, 2ND & 25 AT NE 48
Two plays after a 15-yard penalty for an illegal block, Patrick Mahomes fades back and, under a heavy rush, throws a deep ball to Mecole Hardman, who breaks one tackle, and outrushes another defender to the end zone.

2ND QUARTER, 9:37, KC 10-7 | CHIEFS BALL, 3RD & GOAL AT NE 4
Lining up in a wildcat formation, Travis Kelce takes the direct snap, fakes a handoff to Tyreek Hill, then finds a hole and runs in for a touchdown.

4TH QUARTER, 1:11, KC 23-16 | PATRIOTS BALL, 4TH & 3 AT KC 5
With the game on the line, Tom Brady looks for Julian Edelman in the end zone, but Bashaud Breeland reaches over Edelman's shoulder to knock away the pass and clinch the win.

90

Dustin Colquitt sported the new AFC West champions' cap; Hill, Alex Okafor, Clark, Jones, Demone Harris (back), Jordan Lucas, and Reggie Ragland celebrated the win; Brady congratulated Mahomes after their third encounter in two seasons.

> *"I have ultimate trust in our defense to go out there and get that stop. They've done it the last few weeks now and they've done it this season at certain points. They've built for these moments and they've built and built and you're seeing the results of it now."*
>
> —QUARTERBACK PATRICK MAHOMES

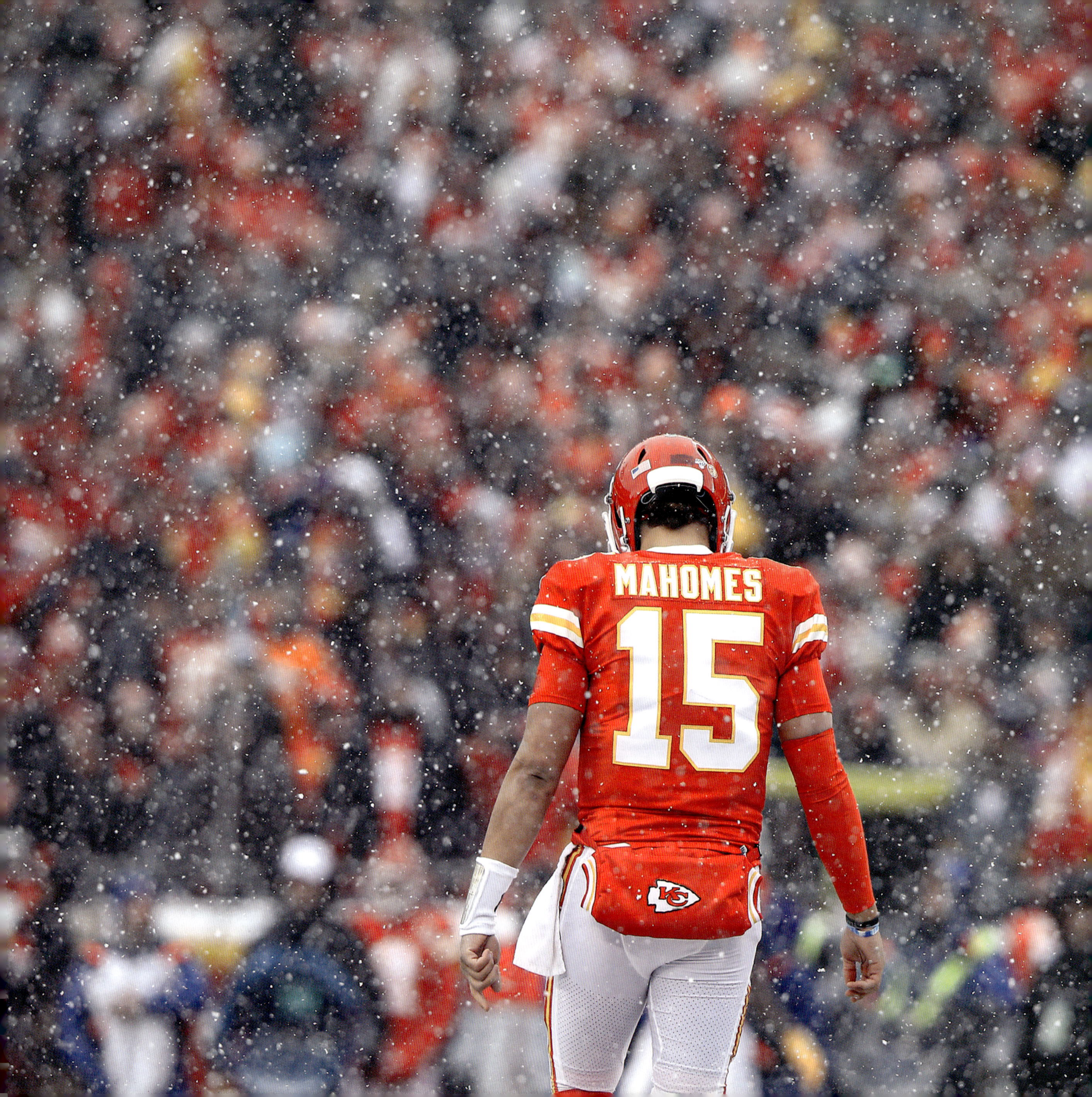
MAHOMES
15

GAME 14 | DECEMBER 15, 2019, AT ARROWHEAD

WINTER WONDERLAND

CHIEFS 23, BRONCOS 3

Having punched their playoff ticket with the big win in New England, the Chiefs returned home intent on remaining alive in the race for the coveted No. 2 seed. On Saturday, they got a pep talk from former Chiefs coach Dick Vermeil. On Sunday, in the midst of one of the biggest gameday snowstorms in Arrowhead history, Patrick Mahomes proved his pregame assertion, "I can spin it in anything," throwing for 340 yards overall, including two touchdown passes to Tyreek Hill, who also led the team in snow angels.

Mahomes proved he could be just as potent in any kind of weather.

THE GAME STORY · The Chiefs defeated the Denver Broncos in a heavy snowstorm, behind a strong showing by the defense and a two-touchdown performance by wide receiver Tyreek Hill.

Hill hauled in a 41-yard score from quarterback Patrick Mahomes on Kansas City's first drive, providing the Chiefs with an early lead, before returning to the end zone midway through the third quarter on a 5-yard touchdown grab.

It marked Hill's seventh game with multiple touchdown receptions since 2017, the most of any player in the NFL.

Kicker Harrison Butker added three field goals in-between Hill's two scores, helping Kansas City build a formidable lead, while the Kansas City defense held Denver to just three points and 251 yards of total offense.

The Broncos went just two-of-seven on third down with 101 yards of offense amid the snowy conditions at Arrowhead in the first half, and that trend continued throughout the second half as safety Juan Thornhill picked off Broncos' quarterback Drew Lock in the end zone to thwart a Denver scoring opportunity.

The defense later held on two fourth-down attempts by the Broncos' offense, preventing Denver from ever putting together a late rally. It marked the fourth-straight game that Kansas City yielded fewer than 20 points defensively.

Mahomes completed 27-of-34 passes for 340 yards and two touchdowns in the victory, finding tight end Travis Kelce 11 times for 142 yards. It was the best statistical performance of the season for Kelce, who surpassed 1,000 receiving yards for the season.

Kelce, the first tight end in the history of the NFL to record four-straight 1,000-yard campaigns, also passed Jimmy Graham for the most receiving yards by a tight end through their first seven seasons in league history.

Kelce was one of six pass-catchers to record double-digit yardage as Kansas City notched its ninth-straight victory over Denver and moved to 26-3 vs. the AFC West since 2015.

—MATT McMULLEN

Hill had two touchdown catches on the day; Tyrann Mathieu batted away a potential touchdown catch by Denver's Courtland Sutton.

"Being committed to getting better every week, every day. Coming into the building with the mindset that no matter what, where we are at now, we are still going to focus on getting better. I feel like we have done that throughout the week, throughout the season, progressing every week."

—DEFENSIVE LINEMAN CHRIS JONES, ON THE KEYS TO THE DEFENSE'S IMPROVEMENT

Jones and the Chiefs defense allowed the Broncos just nine points in two games.

Kelce and Mahomes on the field after the win.

THE BIG PLAYS

1ST QUARTER, 9:50, 0-0 | CHIEFS BALL, 1ST & 10 AT DEN 41
On just their fifth play from scrimmage, Patrick Mahomes finds Tyreek Hill, behind the Broncos secondary, on a deep pass for a touchdown, giving the Chiefs the early 6-0 lead.

2ND QUARTER, 2:11, KC 12-0 | BRONCOS BALL, 2ND & GOAL AT KC 12
With Denver driving late in the half, Drew Lock finds Courtland Sutton in the end zone, but Tyrann Mathieu knocks the ball out of his hands before he can secure the catch, and Denver must settle for three.

3RD QUARTER, 9:50, KC 15-0 | CHIEFS BALL, 1ST & GOAL AT DEN 5
Mahomes rolls left and finds Hill with a short pass, and he slides into the end zone, completing a 10-play, 75-yard touchdown drive to open the second half.

"Coach Vermeil did a great job and I had him talk to the guys yesterday. He went all the way from 'You guys are soft and you don't have to work like we used to work, keeping the pads on through Friday,' to 'You know you got a great football team, and you can be great by putting the hammer down every week. It's not a one-week thing.' I think the guys took it to heart. They gave him a standing ovation. It was pretty good."

—HEAD COACH ANDY REID, ON DICK VERMEIL'S SATURDAY NIGHT TEAM TALK

The statue of team founder Lamar Hunt stood vigil outside Arrowhead; Reid exhorted his team to yet another big divisional victory.

GAME 15 | DECEMBER 22, 2019, AT CHICAGO

CRUISE CONTROL
CHIEFS 26, BEARS 3

On the road at Soldier Field, against a 2018 playoff team coached by former Chiefs' assistant Matt Nagy, Kansas City's offense moved quickly to establish control, the defense suffocated the Bears' attack, and the special teams contributed as well—with kicker Harrison Butker setting another career mark—in a victory that never felt much in doubt. Kansas City went 7-1 away from home, the NFL's best road record. With the holidays and the playoffs just around the corner, the Chiefs were hitting their stride, playing well in all three phases of the game.

With the game well in hand, Hill, Demarcus Robinson, and Mahomes relaxed on the bench.

"I think we are able to wreck a game. We control football games and that is what we have been trying to do, especially defensively. We have been trying to play aggressively, and put teams in bad situations. We have been doing a good job of that."

—SAFETY TYRANN MATHIEU

Mahomes's 12-yard touchdown run put the Chiefs on the board; Kelce's second-quarter touchdown reception led to a 17–0 halftime lead; Jones sacked Trubisky for a 13-yard loss in the fourth quarter.

THE GAME STORY · The Chiefs defeated the Bears at Soldier Field, behind a stifling effort by the defense and a strong performance by quarterback Patrick Mahomes.

Kansas City raced out to a 17-point lead, holding Chicago scoreless until the final seconds of the third quarter, to secure at least 11 victories for the fifth time in seven seasons under head coach Andy Reid.

Mahomes completed 23-of-33 passes for 251 yards and two touchdowns, scrambling for a 12-yard score on Kansas City's first possession before finding tight end Travis Kelce on a 6-yard touchdown strike late in the first half.

Kicker Harrison Butker added a 56-yard field goal between Mahomes's first two scores, a new personal best for him, and the Chiefs' longest field goal since 1985.

Kansas City was back in the end zone midway through the fourth quarter as Mahomes found tailback Damien Williams for a 14-yard score to extend the advantage, and while the offense was building its lead, the defense prevented Chicago from getting much going all night long.

The Bears made it beyond Kansas City's 25-yard line just once, tallying 234 total yards of offense. Defensive end Frank Clark, defensive lineman Chris Jones, and linebacker Reggie Ragland each notched sacks on Bears' quarterback Mitchell Trubisky as part of the impressive effort. The game also featured the debut of Terrell Suggs, claimed off waivers from Arizona earlier in the week.

Offensively, Kelce hauled in eight catches for 74 yards, reaching 500 career receptions in just 95 career games, faster than any tight end in NFL history. Mahomes, meanwhile, reached a milestone of his own by becoming the first player in league history to accumulate both 9,000 passing yards and 75 touchdowns in 30 games or less.

Additionally, wide receiver Tyreek Hill, who had 72 yards on five catches, notched a record by reaching the 4,000-yard receiving mark faster than any player in franchise history.

All three players contributed to Kansas City's fifth victory in a row and seventh road win of the year, marking the Chiefs' most road victories since 1966.

—MATT McMULLEN

THE BIG PLAYS

1ST QUARTER, 3:32, 0-0 | CHIEFS BALL, 3RD & 18 AT CHI 47
Patrick Mahomes fires a dart to Tyreek Hill in the middle of the field for 19 yards, to sustain the Chiefs' opening touchdown drive.

1ST QUARTER, 1:37, 0-0 | CHIEFS BALL, 3RD & 5 AT CHI 12
Mahomes fades back and, finding his receivers covered, takes off toward the corner pylon, sprinting in for the opening score.

2ND QUARTER, 0:56, KC 10-0 | CHIEFS BALL, 1ST & GOAL AT CHI 6
Travis Kelce fakes a sideline route, then angles back inside, and Mahomes finds him with a quick slant pass for a touchdown, to put the Chiefs up by three scores before halftime.

Andy Reid congratulates Clark after another defensive stand.

Mitchell Schwartz, Laurent Duvernay-Tardif, and Austin Reiter kept Mahomes well-protected; rookie Juan Thornhill had three tackles in another strong game.

"We are the Chiefs for a reason. We are the best offense in the league for a reason. That's what we do. This isn't anything new to us. Coming toward the end of the year, our chemistry is coming back from last year, the bonding from all of us. It's all fun. It's been like that, we just had to find it."

—WIDE RECEIVER TYREEK HILL

103

Hardman's kickoff return for a touchdown put the Chiefs ahead to stay.

GAME 16 | DECEMBER 29, 2019, AT ARROWHEAD

SEASON'S GREETINGS
CHIEFS 31, CHARGERS 21

Some had argued that the Chiefs should rest starters for the regular-season finale, since they'd need both a win and a highly unlikely Patriots home loss to the lowly Dolphins to improve their playoff seeding. But Andy Reid kept talking about focusing only on what the team could control. In another hard-fought division battle, the Chiefs prevailed over a gallant Philip Rivers (playing his last game as a Charger), and then—as the clock wound down—a delighted murmur went up from the crowd, and soon built to a roar. A late Christmas gift arrived from Foxborough—and suddenly the Chiefs had a playoff bye week.

THE GAME STORY · Leading by three points and facing a third down with just over four minutes remaining, Chiefs' quarterback Patrick Mahomes found wide receiver Tyreek Hill for a 47-yard completion downfield to move the chains, setting up a game-sealing touchdown a few plays later.

It marked yet another explosive play in a day defined by them, which included a 104-yard kickoff return for a touchdown by rookie wide receiver Mecole Hardman and an 84-yard score by tailback Damien Williams, as Kansas City moved to 27-3 against divisional opponents since 2015.

The winning-effort marked the Chiefs' second-straight season with 12 or more victories—a first in franchise history—as Kansas City, paired with a New England Patriots' loss, locked up the No. 2 seed and a first-round bye in the postseason.

Mahomes completed 16-of-25 passes for 174 yards and a touchdown in the game, finding wide receiver Demarcus Robinson for a 24-yard score late in the second quarter to lift Kansas City out of an early deficit and take the lead.

Los Angeles then recaptured the advantage soon after the second half got underway, but Hardman brought the ensuing kickoff back for a touchdown to push the Chiefs ahead for good.

Williams later extended the lead with his 84-yard touchdown dash, bouncing off would-be tacklers before sprinting down the sideline for his second rushing score of at least 80 yards on the season.

And while Kansas City was building its lead, the defense continued its stellar play of late. Safety Tyrann Mathieu was right in the middle of that effort, tallying his fourth interception of the year to thwart a Chargers' scoring bid. Defensive end Frank Clark, defensive end Terrell Suggs, and defensive lineman Chris Jones each notched a sack.

The Chargers rallied late, pulling to within three points with just over five minutes left in the game, but Mahomes found Hill on Kansas City's ensuing drive before Williams punched in another score to secure the win.

—MATT McMULLEN

Recent signee Suggs earned his first sack as a Chief; no one—save Hill—was catching up with Williams on his long touchdown run.

"I saw Fish do a great job kicking the guy out so all I could do was hit the hole as hard as I could, which is why I was breaking all of those tackles. I trusted my O-line, you know, to hit it with velocity."

—RUNNING BACK DAMIEN WILLIAMS, ON THE ERIC FISHER BLOCK THAT LED TO HIS TOUCHDOWN RUN

Chiefs running backs Anthony Sherman, Darwin Thompson, Williams, and LeSean McCoy are joined by position coach Deland McCullough.

"Swagger. This team plays with tremendous swag. It's a confidence. That's the number one edge that a football player has—confidence. When you have a team that's playing with swagger, and the head ball coach is encouraging that and your position coach is encouraging that, that can help you in January in playoff football."

—DEFENSIVE END TERRELL SUGGS, ON WHAT HE MOST NOTICED ABOUT HIS NEW TEAM

Andy Reid gathered the team for a postgame prayer.

THE BIG PLAYS

3RD QUARTER, 13:14, LAC 14–10 | CHARGERS KICKOFF

Mecole Hardman takes the kick 4 yards deep in his own end zone, follows his blocking toward the left sideline on the return, then cuts back and beats the Chargers to the goal line, to give the Chiefs a lead they wouldn't relinquish.

3RD QUARTER, 6:41, KC 17–14 | CHIEFS BALL, 1ST & 10 AT KC 16

Damien Williams takes a handoff, breaks two tackles near the line of scrimmage, spins free, and races down the sideline 84 yards to put the Chiefs up by two scores.

4TH QUARTER, 0:24, NE 24–20 | DOLPHINS BALL, 1ST & GOAL AT NE 5

A mere 1,411 miles away from Arrowhead, Ryan Fitzpatrick hits Mike Gesicki with a last-minute touchdown pass as the Dolphins shock New England, allowing the Chiefs to claim the No. 2 seed.

Jones celebrated with fans after the game.

GAME 17 | JANUARY 12, 2020, AT ARROWHEAD

GHOST BUSTERS

AFC DIVISIONAL PLAYOFF
CHIEFS 51, TEXANS 31

The Chiefs and their fans knew all about the history of haunted January days when playoff dreams ended in despair. Yet no one could have envisioned this: A season of hope and resilience suddenly facing an incomprehensible 24–0 deficit. But this version of the Chiefs was both supremely talented and mentally tough. And when, early in the second quarter, Mecole Hardman took a kickoff at the goal line and returned it 58 yards, a mighty roar rose up in Arrowhead. The fuse had been lit, and the explosion that followed marked the greatest comeback in franchise history.

Kelce's first of three touchdown catches brought the Chiefs within 10.

"I was thinking we need to score some points."

—HEAD COACH ANDY REID, ASKED WHAT HE WAS THINKING WHEN THE CHIEFS WERE DOWN, 24–0

THE GAME STORY · Chiefs' quarterback Patrick Mahomes completed 23-of-35 passes for 321 yards and five touchdowns in the Chiefs' remarkable comeback victory, finding tight end Travis Kelce for three scores. Tailback Damien Williams also tallied three overall touchdowns in the win. It all helped Kansas City record the fourth-largest comeback in postseason history.

Houston raced out to an enormous lead, scoring 24 unanswered points to begin the game. The Texans capitalized on a blocked punt and a fumble to build their advantage, putting Kansas City in an early hole.

The tide began to turn early in the second quarter, however, as return man Mecole Hardman brought the Texans' kickoff back 58 yards deep into Houston territory. Mahomes then found tailback Damien Williams on a 17-yard score for the Chiefs' first points.

The Texans then ran a failed fake punt on their ensuing drive, turning the ball over on downs to set Kansas City up in great field position, and the Chiefs didn't waste it as Mahomes connected with Kelce for a 5-yard scoring strike.

On the following kickoff, safety Daniel Sorensen—who'd already made the crucial tackle on the fake punt—forced the ball free from Texans' return man DeAndre Carter and into the arms of Chiefs' tailback Darwin Thompson, again providing Kansas City with optimal field position.

Mahomes connected with Kelce yet again just three plays later on a 6-yard touchdown, pulling the Chiefs within a field goal and marking a 21-point explosion in under four minutes of game time.

On their next possession, Mahomes found Kelce for a third time on a 5-yard touchdown to finish off an eight-play, 90-yard scoring drive. After trailing by 24 with 10:54 left in the second quarter, the Chiefs carried the lead into halftime.

Kansas City just kept it coming as the second half got underway, too. Williams rushed for a pair of scores in the third quarter, making it 41 unanswered points for the Chiefs. Though the Texans mustered a third-quarter touchdown, Kansas City responded with 10 more points to seal the game. Playing without standout lineman Chris Jones, the Chiefs' defense had five sacks, three from defensive end Frank Clark.

—MATT McMULLEN

Hardman's kickoff return swung the momentum; Tyrann Mathieu and the defense stiffened after the early onslaught; Williams's touchdown reception began the historic comeback.

THE BIG PLAYS

2ND QUARTER, 10:55, HOU 24-0 |
TEXANS KICK OFF INTO END ZONE

Mecole Hardman fires up the shell-shocked Arrowhead faithful with a 58-yard kickoff return.

2ND QUARTER, 8:32, HOU 24-7 |
TEXANS BALL, 4TH & 4 AT HOU 31

The Texans try a fake punt, with Justin Reid taking the direct snap, but Daniel Sorensen moves in to make the open-field tackle short of the marker, giving the Chiefs the ball.

2ND QUARTER, 8:08, HOU 24-14 |
CHIEFS KICKOFF INTO END ZONE

Sorensen's jarring tackle of DeAndre Carter knocks the ball loose and Darwin Thompson recovers, returning the ball to the Houston 18.

2ND QUARTER, 3:02, HOU 24-21 |
TEXANS BALL, 3RD & 12 AT KC 48

Deshaun Watson finds DeAndre Hopkins over the middle with a pass that would be enough for the first down, but Tyrann Mathieu defends, knocking the ball free for an incomplete pass.

2ND QUARTER, 0:50, HOU 24-21 |
CHIEFS BALL, 3RD & GOAL AT HOU 5

Scrambling under pressure, Mahomes moves toward the line of scrimmage but drags his left foot to keep part of his body behind the line, throwing another touchdown strike to Kelce.

Clockwise from right, Sorensen's tackle of Justin Reid on a fake punt was immense; later he forced a Carter fumble; Clark had three sacks; Eric Fisher celebrated one score with a beer shower.

"He is one of the best special teams players in the world. He has been for most of his career. What else do you expect from him? I don't expect nothing else but greatness from him."

—DEFENSIVE END FRANK CLARK ON TEAMMATE DANIEL SORENSEN

Mahomes's third touchdown pass to Kelce gave the Chiefs the lead just before halftime, prompting another end zone celebration.

> "You see teams that don't have an MVP at quarterback and the skill guys we do, and you say that you want to get them in passing situations. I don't think anyone approaches us and says, 'We want to make them throw the ball.' It definitely plays to a strength of ours in a weird way. I don't think the attitude or mindset really changes, but Coach dials them up, guys get open, and Pat's always going to make incredible plays."
>
> —TACKLE MITCHELL SCHWARTZ

TOUCHDOWN

Demarcus Robinson reacted right along with the Arrowhead faithful to Mahomes's spectacular scramble for a touchdown.

GAME 18 | JANUARY 19, 2020, AT ARROWHEAD

HOMECOMING

AFC CHAMPIONSHIP GAME
CHIEFS 35, TITANS 24

The trophy given to the winner of the American Football Conference championship game was renamed in honor of Lamar Hunt in 1984. But the Chiefs had never won the prize named after their founder. On this day, decades of frustration were wiped away by a resourceful offense, a spirited and tenacious defense, and one of the great quarterback scrambles in playoff history. At the end of the day, as confetti and raucous cheers floated around Arrowhead, the Lamar Hunt Trophy was in the possession of the Kansas City Chiefs. And it was time to make travel plans for Miami.

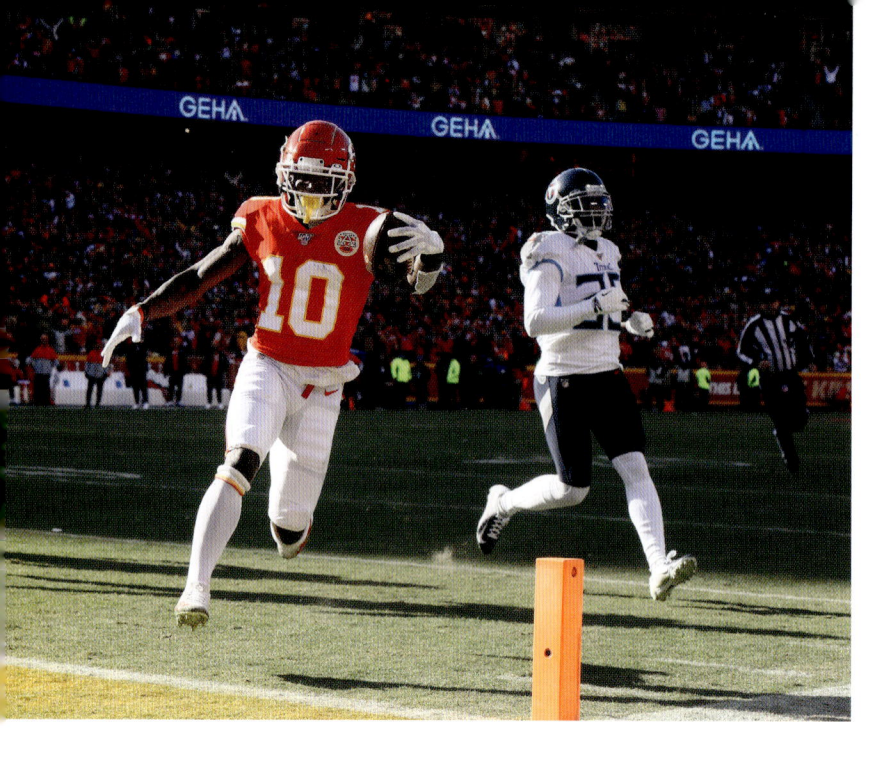

THE GAME STORY · The Kansas City Chiefs defeated the Tennessee Titans, 35–24, at Arrowhead Stadium to advance to the Super Bowl for the first time in 50 years.

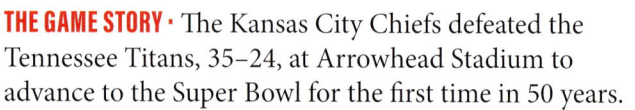

Kansas City fought back from an early deficit to tally 28 unanswered points, establishing a commanding lead while preventing Tennessee from ever getting back into the game.

Chiefs' quarterback Patrick Mahomes completed 23-of-35 passes for 294 yards and three touchdowns in the game, finding wide receiver Tyreek Hill for a pair of scores in the first half to help Kansas City climb out of the early hole.

After falling behind by 10 points midway through the first quarter, Mahomes tossed the ball to Hill, who was sweeping to his left, on a quick "pop pass" before the speedy Hill turned the corner and dashed ahead for an 8-yard score.

The Titans then answered the Chiefs' score with a touchdown of their own, but Hill was back in the end zone a possession later when Mahomes fired a laser up the seam and into Hill's outstretched arms 20 yards downfield to narrow the deficit.

Kansas City proceeded to force a three-and-out on the Titans' next series, setting up a third-consecutive scoring drive by the Chiefs that ended in a 27-yard, go-ahead scoring scramble by Mahomes in the final seconds of the first half.

That score held throughout the entirety of the third quarter before tailback Damien Williams plunged ahead for a 4-yard touchdown to extend the Chiefs' advantage early in the fourth quarter.

Mahomes then found wide receiver Sammy Watkins for a 60-yard touchdown a drive later, putting Kansas City up by three scores. Tennessee chipped away at the deficit late, as Titans' quarterback Ryan Tannehill found tight end Anthony Firkser for a 22-yard touchdown with just over four minutes remaining.

Mahomes finished the game with 53 yards on the ground while Hill and Watkins each had productive days through the air. Watkins, in particular, hauled in seven catches for a team-leading 114 yards.

Defensively, defensive end Tanoh Kpassagnon tallied a pair of sacks as the Chiefs held Tennessee scoreless from midway through the second quarter until Firkser's score late in the fourth quarter. Kansas City held Titans' tailback Derrick Henry, who had at least 180 rushing yards in each of Tennessee's previous two postseason games, to just 69 yards on the ground.

It all helped Kansas City defeat Tennessee and hoist the Lamar Hunt Trophy for the first time in franchise history.

—MATT McMULLEN

"They have big hearts. So, they work hard and never give up. They're going to give you four quarters of honest football, every snap. I appreciate that. They don't care about the score; they just bring it. That's paid off for us the last couple of weeks."

—HEAD COACH ANDY REID, ASKED ABOUT THE TEAM'S IDENTITY

Hill brought a short pass into the end zone to give the Chiefs their first points; Williams's fourth-quarter touchdown put them up by 11; Clark Hunt was joined at the drum by '69 Chiefs greats Willie Lanier, Bobby Bell, and Jan Stenerud; Watkins's 60-yard touchdown reception started the celebration.

"In the NFL you are going to go through adversity. Learning that last year, obviously the loss hurt, but having to watch the Super Bowl and not being in it, was something I could barely even do. For me, I knew I wanted to be in this moment. I think that's what we preached as a team; we want to be here. We want to be in the Super Bowl but we have to take advantage of every single day that we get."

—QUARTERBACK PATRICK MAHOMES

THE BIG PLAYS

1ST QUARTER, 2:58, TEN 10-0 | CHIEFS BALL, 4TH & 2 AT TEN 28
Patrick Mahomes finds Travis Kelce for a 4-yard gain and a first down to keep alive the Chiefs' initial touchdown drive.

2ND QUARTER, 4:07, TEN 17-7 | CHIEFS BALL, 2ND & 10 AT TEN 20
Mahomes threads a pass down the middle to Tyreek Hill in tight coverage, bringing the Chiefs back to within a field goal.

2ND QUARTER, 0:23, TEN 17-14 | CHIEFS BALL, 2ND & 10 AT TEN 27
Mahomes eludes two rushers and heads for the left sideline, then tightropes down the field before cutting inside and running through another tackle en route to a go-ahead touchdown.

3RD QUARTER, 7:54, KC 21-17 | TITANS BALL, 3RD & 8 AT TEN 38
Ryan Tannehill scrambles out of the pocket into the open field, racing for the first-down marker, but Daniel Sorensen closes him down and tackles him cleanly 2 yards short.

4TH QUARTER, 7:44, KC 28-17 | CHIEFS BALL, 3RD & 6 AT KC 40
Mahomes fades back and finds Sammy Watkins streaking down the middle of the field, beyond the Titans' secondary, and hits him in stride for the touchdown that puts the game out of reach.

The Chiefs defense limited Henry to just 69 yards; new defensive leaders Frank Clark and Tyrann Mathieu both had big days.

As Arrowhead erupted in confetti, Mahomes faced the media throng, before the AFC champions gathered in the celebratory locker room.

"A few years ago, I think it was around Super Bowl 50, after my mom had been to 50 Super Bowls, she said, 'Clark, it sure would be nice if we could play in this game once while I'm still able to go.' We've got that checked off but at the end of the day, we've still got a big goal to accomplish . . . Our big goal left is to bring another Lombardi trophy back to Kansas City."

—CHAIRMAN CLARK HUNT

The Hunt family and the city cheered as Clark Hunt raised the trophy named after his father.

GAME 19 | FEBRUARY 2, 2020, IN MIAMI

SUPER CHIEFS

SUPER BOWL LIV
CHIEFS 31, 49ERS 20

On the biggest stage in American sports, the Kansas City Chiefs completed one of the most remarkable playoff runs in the history of pro football. For the third game in a row, they found themselves trailing by double digits—this time in the fourth quarter, not the first—and once again they stormed back to a convincing victory. Fifty years after "65 Toss Power Trap" highlighted the Chiefs win in Super Bowl IV, a play called "Jet Chip Wasp" would become the signature play of Super Bowl LIV. And at the end of the National Football League's 100th season—just as in the 50th—the Chiefs reigned as world champions.

Mahomes, after taking a deep drop, launched the crucial throw to Hill some 55 yards in the air.

Hill's 44-yard gain sparked the fourth-quarter rally; Sammy Watkins eluded the 49ers Richard Sherman for a key catch on the go-ahead drive.

"You know, we were down 20-10 and he was telling us to believe in the fourth quarter. He saw it in some guys' eyes, they were getting down, including myself. I was like, 'Man, how are we going to pull this off?' and he was like, '10, you've got to believe, brother. Like the same faith you've had all of your career, you've got to believe right now. It's going to happen, man; I can feel it.' He brought the guys together, and you saw what happened."

—WIDE RECEIVER TYREEK HILL, ON PATRICK MAHOMES'S SIDELINE DEMEANOR

THE GAME STORY · Trailing by 10 points with just under nine minutes remaining, Chiefs' quarterback Patrick Mahomes led Kansas City to 21 unanswered points to win the franchise's second Super Bowl title.

Mahomes first found tight end Travis Kelce for a 1-yard touchdown to narrow the deficit before slinging a 5-yard score to tailback Damien Williams for the Chiefs' first lead since midway through the second quarter.

It was then up to the defense to protect the advantage, and facing a fourth-and-10 at midfield, defensive end Frank Clark sacked 49ers' quarterback Jimmy Garoppolo to effectively secure the victory. The Chiefs took back over offensively, and Williams found the end zone yet again on a 38-yard touchdown scamper to seal it.

The 24-year-old Mahomes, named the game's MVP, became the second-youngest starting quarterback to hoist the Lombardi Trophy in NFL history.

After an early San Francisco field goal, the Chiefs then answered with an outstanding series of their own, stringing together a 15-play, 75-yard drive that culminated in a 1-yard, go-ahead touchdown scramble by Mahomes.

Shortly thereafter, the Chiefs came up with a big play on the other side of the ball, as Bashaud Breeland intercepted an errant pass from Garoppolo. Kicker Harrison Butker connected on a 31-yard field goal to turn the takeaway into points a short while later, extending the Chiefs' advantage. San Francisco knotted things up, however, with a 15-yard scoring strike from Garoppolo to fullback Kyle Juszczyk to tie the game.

The 49ers then took the lead following the break, as kicker Robbie Gould nailed a 42-yard field goal to push San Francisco ahead again, and later extended their advantage to 20-10 on a 1-yard plunge by tailback Raheem Mostert.

After two drives were stopped by interceptions, Kansas City got the ball back with just under nine minutes remaining, setting up a 44-yard connection between Mahomes and wide receiver Tyreek Hill on third-and-15 to move the chains and spark the rally.

The Chiefs moved to 5-0 this season—and 3-0 in the playoffs—when trailing by 10 or more points, the first time ever a team has staged three double-digit comebacks in a single postseason.

—MATT McMULLEN

Mahomes ran it in for the Chiefs' first touchdown, after a busy week of preparation in Miami.

THE BIG PLAYS

1ST QUARTER, 1:57, SF 3-0 | CHIEFS BALL, 4TH & 1 AT SF 5

"Shift to Rose Bowl Right Parade"—the variation of a play run by Michigan in the 1948 Rose Bowl—finds Damien Williams taking the direct snap and charging ahead for 4 yards.

2ND QUARTER, 14:15, KC 7-3 | 49ERS BALL, 2ND & 12 AT SF 40

Chris Jones and Mike Pennel crash the interior line, forcing a hurried throw from Jimmy Garoppolo, intercepted by Bashaud Breeland.

4TH QUARTER, 7:13, SF 20-10 | CHIEFS BALL, 3RD & 15 AT KC 35

The instant classic "Jet Chip Wasp" finds Patrick Mahomes—throwing from nearly 15 yards behind the line of scrimmage—connecting with Tyreek Hill on a ball that traveled more than 50 yards in the air, to bring KC down to the 49ers 21.

4TH QUARTER, 5:27, SF 20-17 | 49ERS BALL, 2ND & 5 AT SF 25

Garoppolo sees George Kittle open beyond the first-down marker in the middle of the field, but his pass is batted down by Jones, one of three passes deflected on the day.

4TH QUARTER, 2:50, SF 20-17 | CHIEFS BALL, 3RD & GOAL AT SF 5

Mahomes rolls out and hits Damien Williams with a short pass, which Williams carries to paydirt, extending the ball over the pylon just before going out of bounds.

Kelce had six catches and a touchdown on the day; Chris Jones harried Garoppolo all game long, deflecting three passes.

Williams reached over the goal line to put the Chiefs ahead to stay in the fourth quarter.

"Don't matter the score. Doesn't matter. We've got Pat Mahomes, we've got an unbelievable defense and they'll put their foot in the ground against anybody saying, 'Enough is enough,' and that is what they did tonight. Coach Andy Reid, baby! We got a ring for Big Red. Can't get rid of us now, Red. You're married to us forever. Forever!"

—TIGHT END TRAVIS KELCE

"I don't know if everybody believed in this defense, even from the beginning of the year. It's been a process and we believed in ourselves. That's the biggest thing. We've got great leadership on this team. Tyrann Mathieu, Frank Clark—those guys have led us and kept talking to us. Believe in ourselves, trust in ourselves, we're going to get better, we're getting better. You see that process and we continued to get better and better and better. When it came down to it, the defense was able to make some key stops and get the offense the ball back and let them do what they do."

—SAFETY DANIEL SORENSEN

Clark's sack of Garoppolo ended one fourth-quarter drive.

Kendall Fuller's interception (above) prompted an on-field celebration; then Williams ran 38 yards for the game-clinching touchdown.

Architect Reid and field general Mahomes shared a hug as the clock wound down, just moments before Reid received his Gatorade victory shower.

"I had two goals when I became the starting quarterback for the Kansas City Chiefs, and the first goal was to win the Lamar Hunt Trophy. I wanted to bring it home, the one that has our founder's name on it. I wanted to bring it to this family and this organization. And the second most important thing was to get Coach Reid a Super Bowl trophy. He's one of the greatest coaches of all time. I don't think he needed the Lombardi Trophy to prove that. But just to do that, it puts all doubt aside, and he's going to be listed as one of the all-time great coaches in history whenever he wants to be done, which I hope is not anytime soon."

—QUARTERBACK PATRICK MAHOMES

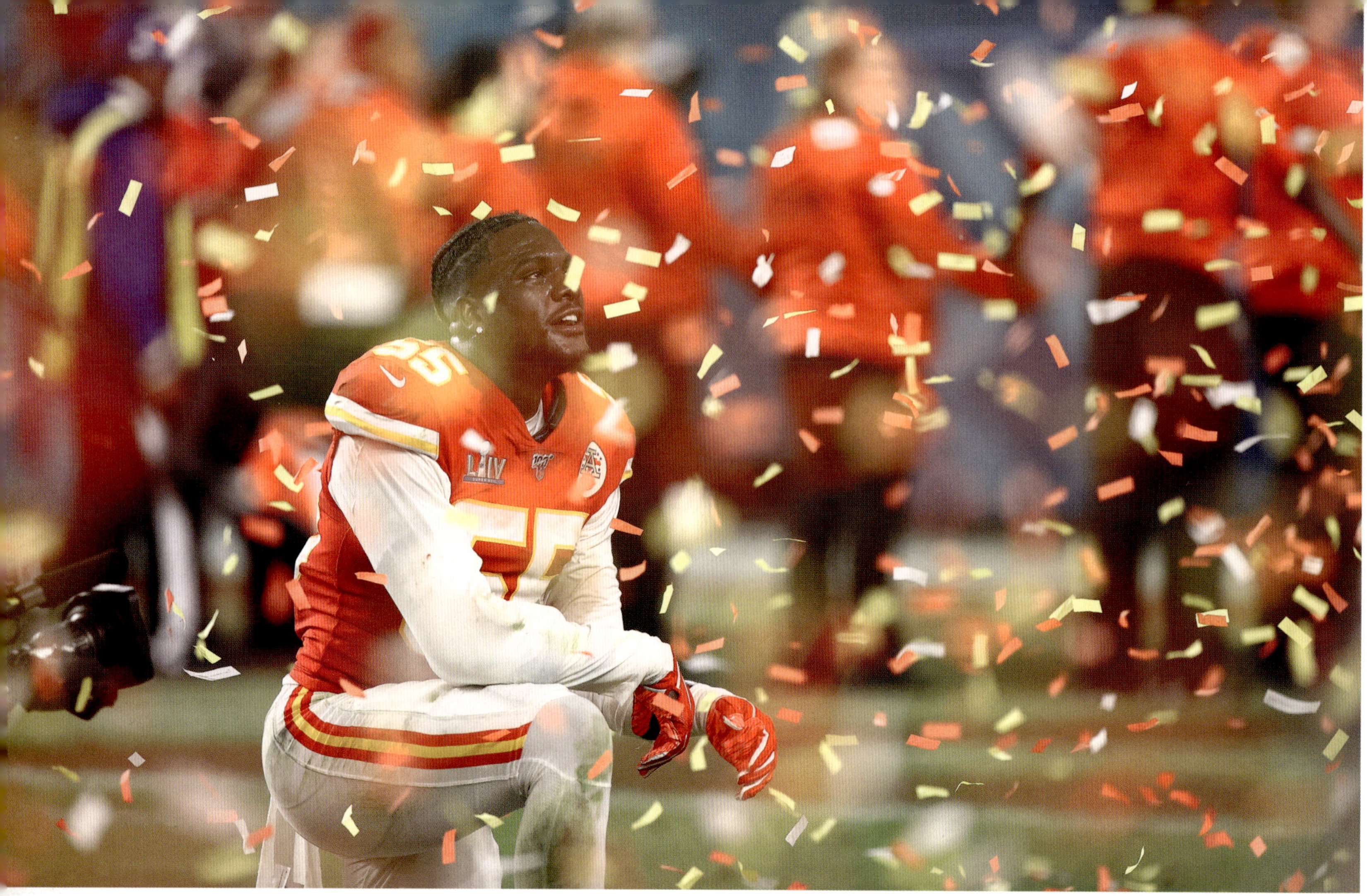
LIV
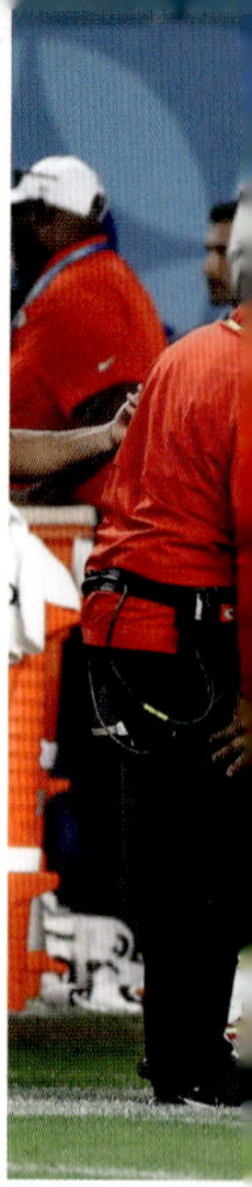
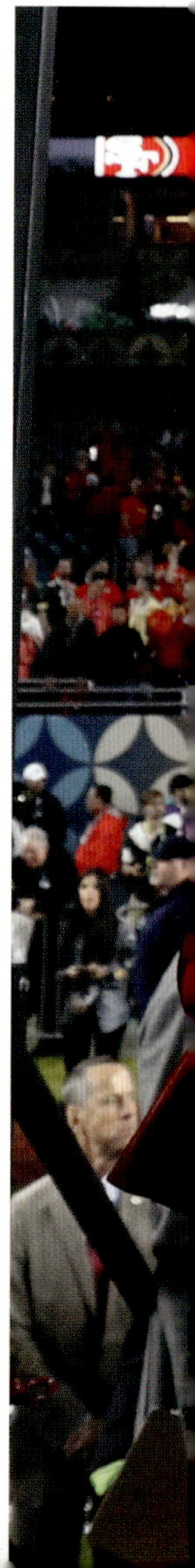
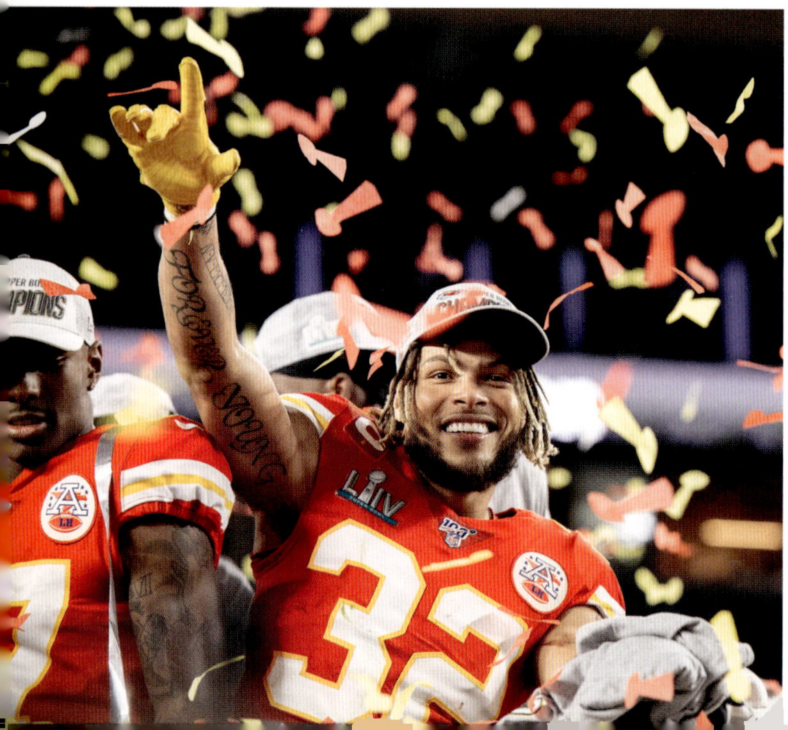
LIV
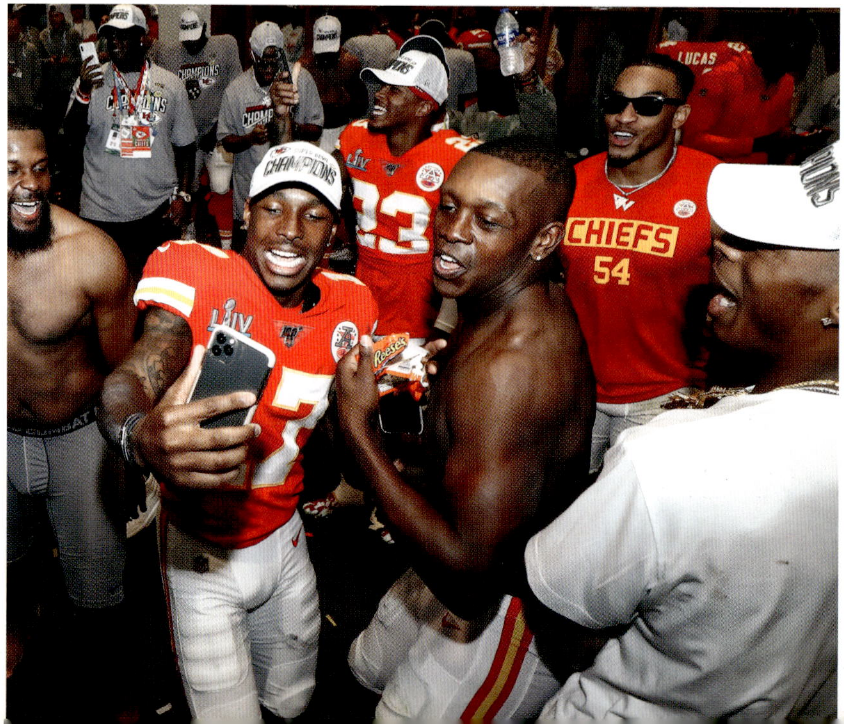
CHAMPIONS
LIV
CHIEFS
54

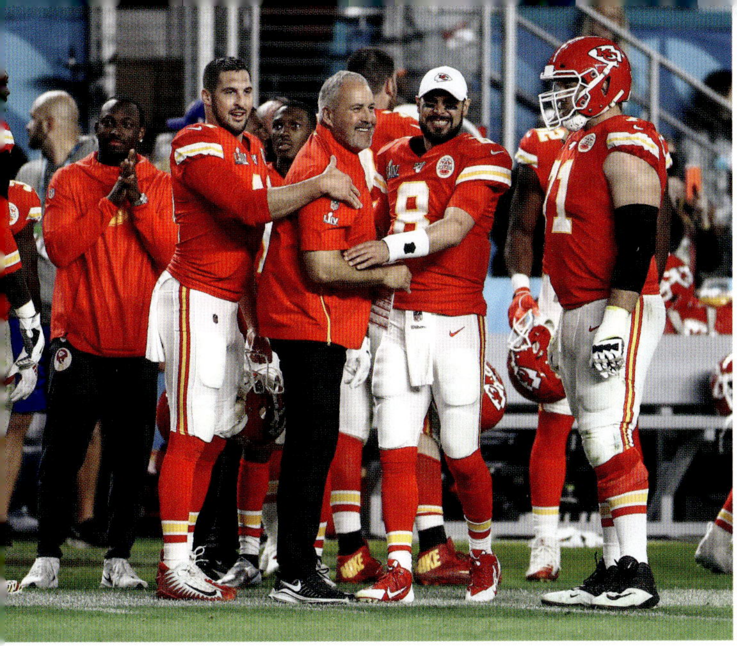

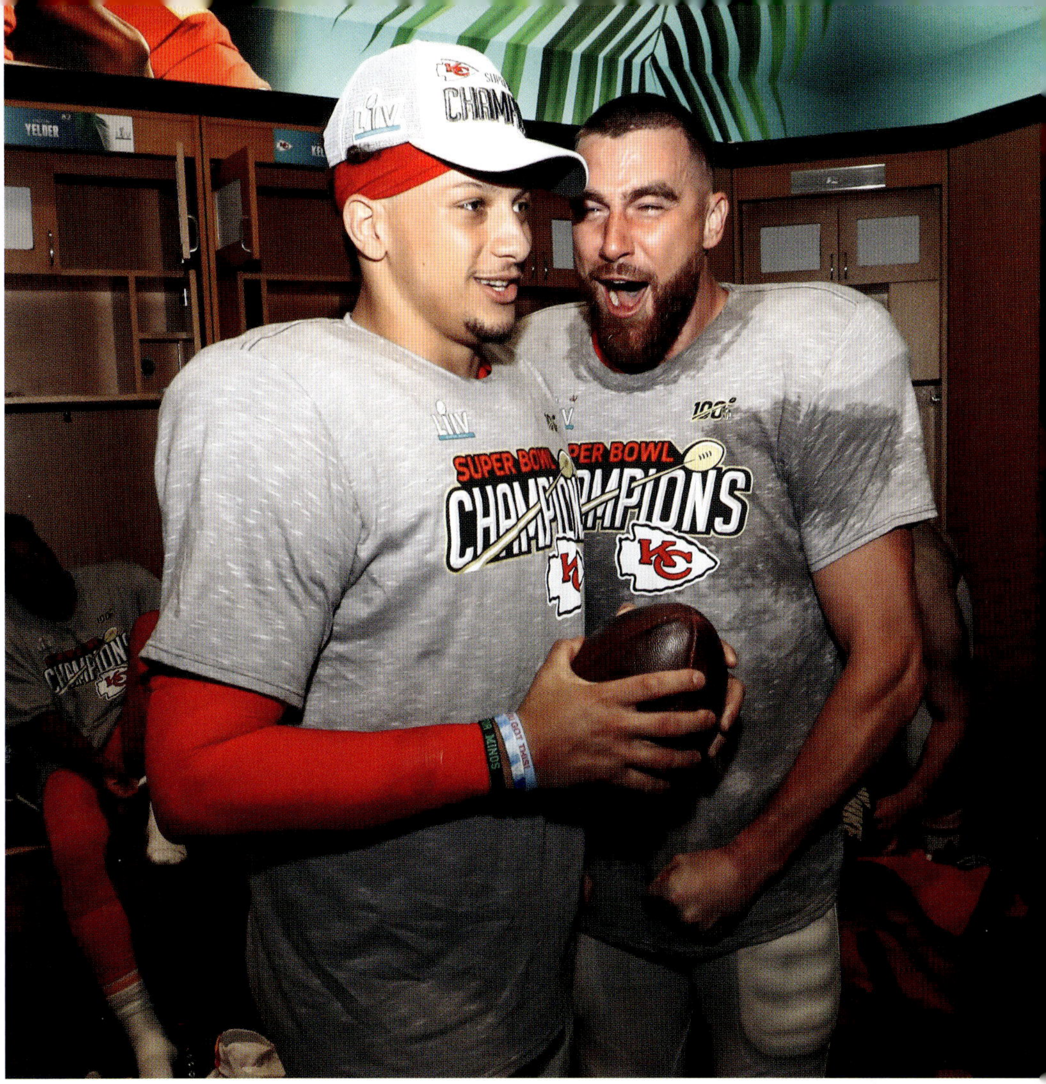

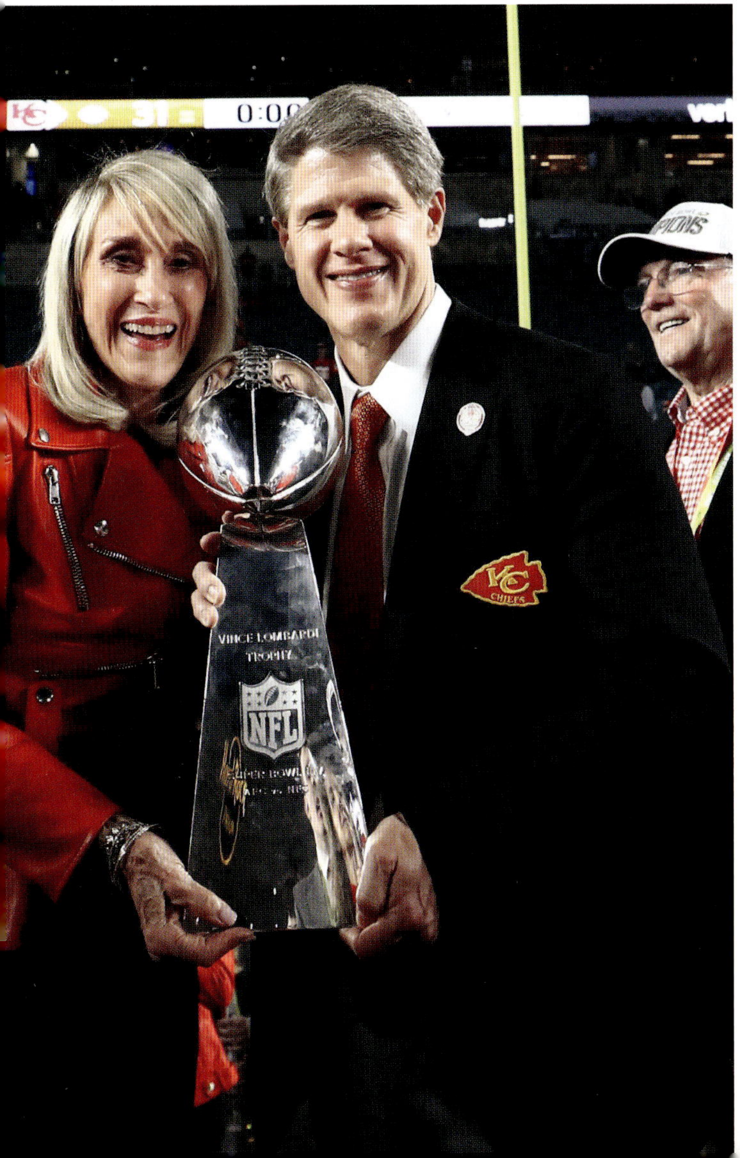
VINCE LOMBARDI
TROPHY
NFL

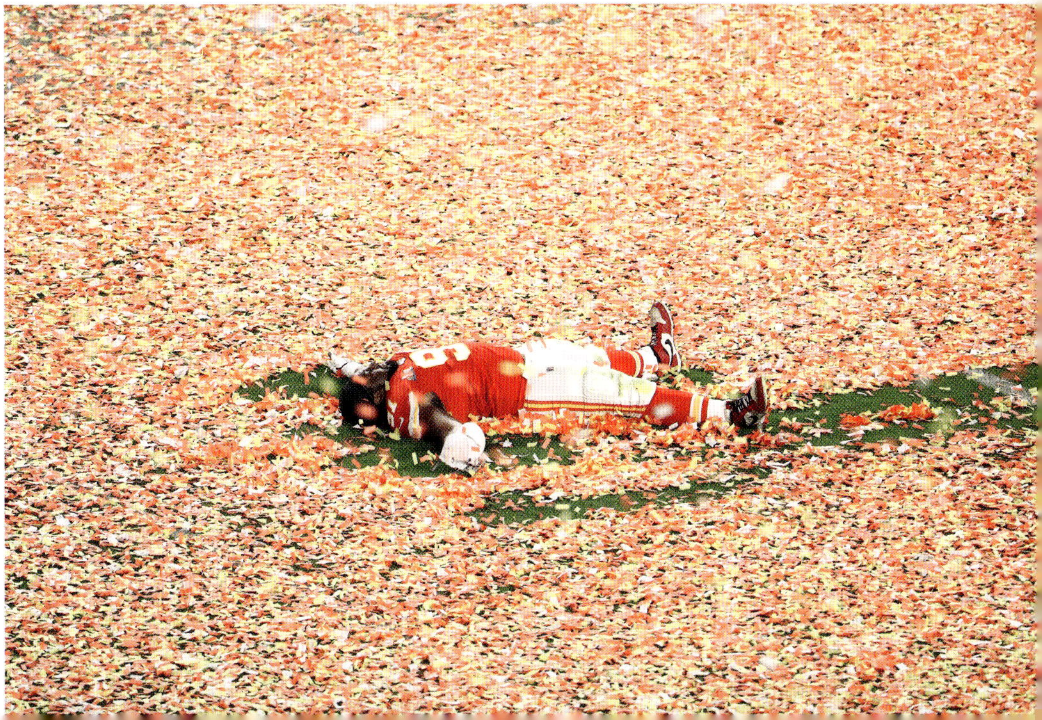

THE PARADE

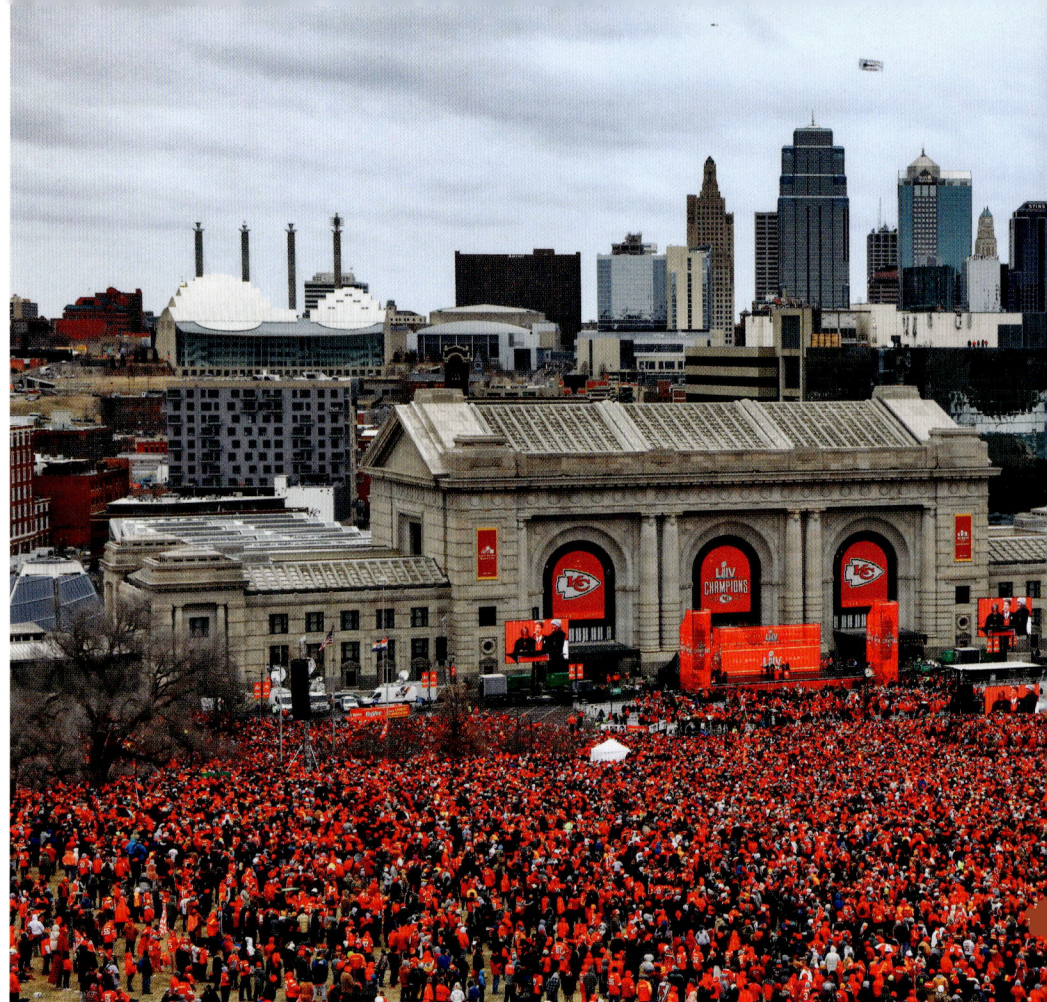

KANSAS CITY Chiefs
SUPER BOWL LIV CHAMPIONS

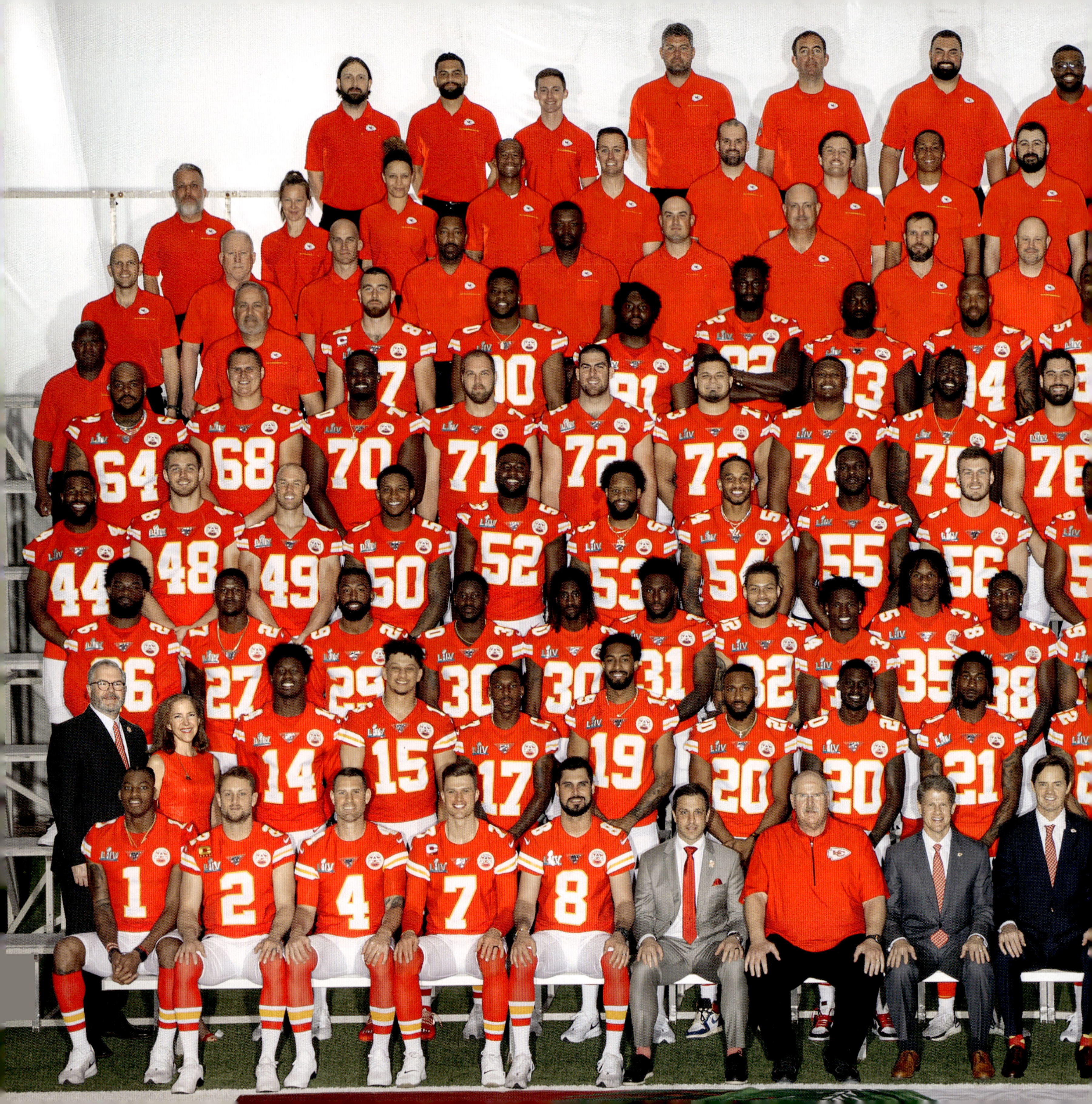

THE TEAM

SUPER BOWL LIV CHAMPION KANSAS CITY CHIEFS

Row 9: Cale Kirby, Connor Embree, Holt McKenney, Jay White, Kyle Crumbaugh, Travis Crittenden, Terry Bradden, Mike Frazier, Ryan Reynolds, Dan Williams.

Row 8: Chris Shropshire, Julie Frymyer, Tiffany Morton, David Glover, Evan Craft, David Girardi, Alex Whittingham, Greg Carbin, Ken Radino, Josh Schmidt, Pat Brazil, Porter Elliett, Barry Rubin, Allen Wright.

Row 7: Corey Matthaei, Tom Melvin, Joe Bleymaier, Greg Lewis, Rod Wilson, Mike Kafka, Andy Heck, Brenden Daly, Matt House, Sam Madison, Britt Reid, Deland McCullough, Dave Merritt, Rick Burkholder.

Row 6: Eric Bieniemy, Dave Toub, Travis Kelce, Emmanuel Ogbah, Derrick Nnadi, Tanoh Kpassagnon, Davaroe Lawrence, Terrell Suggs, Chris Jones, Braxton Hoyett, Alex Okafor, Xavier Williams, Khalen Saunders, Steve Spagnuolo.

Row 5: Mike Pennel, Jackson Barton, Greg Senat, Mitchell Schwartz, Eric Fisher, Nick Allegretti, Martinas Rankin, Cam Erving, Laurent Duvernay-Tardif, Andrew Wylie, Felton Davis, Blake Bell, Deon Yelder.

Row 4: Dorian O'Daniel, Nick Keizer, Daniel Sorensen, Darron Lee, Demone Harris, Anthony Hitchens, Damien Wilson, Frank Clark, Ben Niemann, Reggie Ragland, Ryan Hunter, Stefen Wisniewski, Austin Reiter.

Row 3: Damien Williams, Rashad Fenton, Kendall Fuller, Elijah McGuire, Alex Brown, Darrel Williams, Tyrann Mathieu, Darwin Thompson, Charvarius Ward, Chris Lammons, Spencer Ware, John Lovett, James Winchester, Anthony Sherman, Emmanuel Smith, Mike Weber.

Row 2: Lamar Hunt, Jr., Sharron Hunt, Sammy Watkins, Patrick Mahomes, Mecole Hardman, Marcus Kemp, Keith Reaser, Morris Claiborne, Bashaud Breeland, Juan Thornhill, Armani Watts, Jordan Lucas, LeSean McCoy, Norma Hunt, Dan Hunt.

Row 1: Jody Fortson, Dustin Colquitt, Chad Henne, Harrison Butker, Matt Moore, Brett Veach, Andy Reid, Clark Hunt, Mark Donovan, Kyle Shurmur, Tyreek Hill, Demarcus Robinson, Gehrig Dieter, Byron Pringle.

Helmet worn by Len Dawson, circa 1969.

Helmet worn by Patrick Mahomes, circa 2019.

ACKNOWLEDGMENTS

In 2019, I was finally able to write a book I'd been contemplating for years, about the 1969 Kansas City Chiefs, published on the occasion of the 50th anniversary of their historic world championship season. I remember thinking, as the book was going to press, that there would be a delightful symmetry if the 2019 Chiefs finally returned to the big game for the first time in a half-century. And then it happened.

This is a different sort of book. It's not a sequel, so much as an impressionistic "extended snapshot" of the 2019 season, as a friend of mine described it. But it's been a joy to edit and create, and a labor of love to relive the ebbs and flows of that exhilarating campaign.

This is the third project I've done with Andrews McMeel Publishing, and it was again the right place for this book. Publisher Kirsty Melville understands the value of home field advantage, and I appreciate her confidence in making sure this happened. It was a blast to work side-by-side again (albeit via Zoom) with ace editor Jean Lucas and the gifted designer/art director Spencer Williams. I'm also appreciative of the help from the rest of the team, including production editor Dave Shaw; production manager Carol Coe; marketing maven Kathy Hilliard; Lynne McAdoo, Jaime Cochrane, and Emily Folks of the sales team; and Tiffani Dickinson in the legal department. Additional thanks are owed to Jean's kitchen cabinet of readers: longtime season ticket holder Randy Herr and fervent Chiefs fans (and native Kansas Citians) Jan Flemington and Marti Petty.

I want to thank Clark Hunt and the Kansas City Chiefs for their absolutely essential cooperation on this project. They graciously shared their photographic archive and artifacts to help document the season. A special debt of gratitude is owed to team historian and curmudgeon emeritus Bob Moore, who helped coordinate with the Chiefs the materials needed for this book. We also got valuable assistance along the way from Ryan Petkoff and Alan Tomkins, in the Dallas office; Mike Davidson and Kyle Crumbaugh with the Chiefs; and Dr. Rob Clemens and Jay Roberts. Additionally, I'm appreciative of the ample help provided by Ted Crews and his team in football communications, including Brad Gee, Luke Shanno, Cydney Ricker, and Jordan Trgovac. The book also contains condensed versions of Matt McMullen's game stories, written in the heat of the moment.

I'm particularly grateful to head coach Andy Reid for taking the time and care to write a foreword that is both revealing and moving. It's been clear for a long time that he was the right man for the job; his writing here helps further explain why.

The heart of this book is its splendid, extensive, and diverse photography, and for this I want to commend Chiefs team photographer Steve Sanders and the rest of his band of shooters, including Jim Berry, Andrew Mather, Ben Green, Chris Donahue, Sam Lutz, and Cassie Florido.

Kansas City is my hometown, and I'll always be grateful for my enduring friendships with Laura Pfeifauf, Greg Emas, Katherine and Jay Rivard, Trey Gratwick, Jane and Jonny Girson, Tim and Janice Martin, Stefan Zauchenberger, Dodie Jacobi, and Bob and Mary Jacobi, as well as my "friends in the business" Vahe and Cindy Gregorian, Sam Mellinger, and Blair Kerkhoff.

I also want to thank my regular crew of football-Sunday co-conspirators in Austin: Aaron Cooper, Travis Farley, Natalie Hocharon, and Melissa and Scott Harrington. Thanks as well to fellow (and far-flung) literate Chiefs fans and friends Reggie Givens, Joe Posnanski, Bill James, Grant Wahl, Shekar Sathyanarayana, Ross Lillard, and Ben Meers.

A special thanks to my family: my mother, Lois MacCambridge, my sister and brother-in-law, Angie and Tom Szentgyorgyi, and longtime friends James and Nicole Stubbe, Earl Summers, Riza Rafi, Roger and Leslie Williams, and Nancy Gates, for their support over the years.

For their friendship and wisdom shared along the way, I'm thankful for Pat Porter, Susan Reckers, Rich Moffitt, Akin Owoso, Larry Johnson, Larry Kindbom, Loren Watt, Stan Webb, Chris Brown, Tony Owens, Arlyn Owens, Adam Moses, Steve Bosky, Rusty Kutzer, Lesley McCullough McCallister, Brian Hay, Ryan Cox, George McMahon, Jeff Zivan, Kirk Bohls, Ced Golden, Doug Miller, Mark Rosner, Peter Blackstock, Sam Ulu, Bola Lamidi, David Joiner, and Jacqui Dunleavy. I am forever grateful to Jennifer Harrison for her support and optimism.

My dear friends—and fellow football obsessives—Rob Minter, Kevin Lyttle, and Brad Garrett all viewed earlier versions of this book and offered insight, corrections, and helpful suggestions.

Finally, this book was started and finished amid the COVID-19 lockdown, while I was living in close quarters with my restless college-aged children, Miles and Ella. I am especially grateful to them because they remained, somehow, good company through it all.

—MJM,
AUSTIN, JUNE 2020